C000135238

MURDER, MUTINY AND THE MUGLINS

A TRUE 18th CENTURY SAGA
OFF IRELAND'S COAST

Des Burke-Kennedy

First published 2020

© Des Burke-Kennedy

www.MurderMutinyandtheMuglins.com

Reprinted 2021

Front Cover Photograph:

John Fahy Photographer

Cover Design: Artwerk Limited

With assistance from Titan11Film & More Visual Ltd.

ISBN:

978-1-8382006-0-2 – First Edition (Hardback)

978-1-8382006-1-9 – Second Edition (Hardback)

978-1- 8382006-2-6 – Kindle

978-1- 8382006-4-0 MMM EBook

978-1- 8382006-3-3 – Paperback

All rights reserved. No part of this publication may be reproduced, stored in or introduced into a retrieval system, or transmitted, in any form or by any means (electronic, mechanical, photocopying, recording or otherwise) without the prior written permission of both the copyright owners and the publisher of this book.

DEDICATION

At the time of writing, Ireland, Europe and the world are cocooned or on lockdown in a global effort to combat the deadly Covid-19 virus. I would like to dedicate this book to the families of all whose lives have been cut short by this overwhelming pandemic. By the time you reach the final page of this story, the virus may also have been conquered and a vaccine developed. We live in hope.

— DES BURKE-KENNEDY, APRIL 2020

READERS' COMMENTS

Peter Wallis, Author, Dalkey, Ireland: I have not enjoyed a well written book as much as this for a very long time. I am sure it will soon be a best seller and deserves to be for it is truly excellent.

Dr Michael B. Morgan, Dermatopathologist, Florida, USA: A raconteur the likes of which would render Shakespeare proud, I thoroughly enjoyed how you were able to weave history and reasoned conjecture with such aplomb.

Dublin History Record Magazine, Ireland: This ripping well-recounted story of true crime backed up by solid research is well worth the attention of maritime history buffs, local historians of Dublin and lovers of adventure stories and crime mysteries.

Gareth Davies, Edinburgh, Expert Walking Tours, Scotland: I devoured it over the weekend! What a fantastic story and the research you've done is incredible.

Professor Andrew Burke, Dean & Chair of Business Studies, Trinity College Dublin: I was really impressed with the elegant writing style and rigorous research which helped provide so much detail to the story. It was a really enjoyable read.

Jon Broderick, Publisher, Florida, USA: This book is worthy of being a college text of required reading about period history.

Andrew Leonard, Lighting Director, Dalkey, Ireland: I can see it being snapped up for a movie.

Dr Michael Kennedy RHA, Dublin, Ireland: A fantastic tale and perfect Covid lockdown reading as you transport the reader to foreign parts.

Gill Hill, Fayence, France: It was a very gripping tale and I just loved the final chapters to back up the theory.

Karen Busher, Dundee, Scotland: Once I'd finished, I started over on this book and am currently enjoying my second read of it.

Daphne Matthews, Author, Dalkey, Ireland: It was so powerful I seriously was a little creeped going asleep thinking of all the hangings and also that the bodies travelled around this Dalkey area.

Mick Daniels, Waterford, Ireland: It is a page turner, I enjoyed it immensely and would highly recommend it.

CONTENTS

PREFACE

The story ends in the small seaside heritage town of Dalkey on the south side of Dublin Bay in Ireland. To finally arrive there, the journey could be the stuff of fiction. It is instead a true test of the strength and character of some extraordinary people. Taking place between the years 1695 and 1773, the chilling tale involves events and individuals in Britain, the Canary Islands, Guadeloupe, Senegal, Ireland and a mysterious location referred to as Port Hillsborough. India too is part of our journey. It was a time when violence at sea was often the route to great wealth, when slavery was regarded as an acceptable business and when life expectancy in general was short but in particular for mariners.

To paint a picture of what life was like for many of those associated with seafaring in the 1700s, I have included details of the role played by mariners and their significant impact on international trade, and explored some elements of early technology developments which also impacted life at sea. Travel beyond one's local neighbourhood was often both dangerous and expensive, but in spite of this, some thought little of crossing the Atlantic, rounding the Cape of Good Hope and even reaching the East Indies and China.

Most of all, this is a story of a true adventurer, his brave wife and the risks which they were prepared to take.

My father, Bernard, did something very special for my sister, Janette, and me when we were very young children. By reading many of the classics to us each night before we went to bed, he rippled our imaginations. Those wonderful tales, which created both dreams and nightmares, are still etched in our brains over a half century later. In my mind's eye, I can still see those small brown leather-bound books, part of a collection, with their gold-edged pages, blue ribbon markers attached to their spines and occasional black-and-white drawings. While I have already forgotten some, those I do remember include *The Black Tulip* by Alexandre Dumas, *Rob Roy* by Walter Scott, *The Three Musketeers* by Aleksander Dima, *A Tale of Two Cities* and *David Copperfield* by Charles Dickens, and most of all, *Kidnapped* and *Treasure Island*, the two great Robert Louis Stevenson novels. Rereading Stevenson's books recently made me wonder if they would not frighten the living daylights out of most young children today! Most interestingly, it is conceivable that there might be some connection between Robert Louis Stevenson, the central figure of our story, George Glass, and the Muglins in Dalkey?

Writing this book has opened my eyes to a very different world of two centuries ago. I hope you, too, will feel likewise by the time you reach the final chapter.

DES BURKE-KENNEDY
MOUNT SALUS
DALKEY
APRIL 2020

PROLOGUE

Before we enter upon the bloody deeds of these inhuman monsters, we shall present our readers with an account of the cruel fortune of Captain Glass, who had fought against the enemies of his country; and, after undergoing from them a long series of cruel treatment, at length fell a victim to the abominable cruelty of the pirates.

— *The Newgate Calendar* report, 1765

CHRONOLOGY

1695 Rev John Glas born on 21 September

1713 Rev John Glas graduates from University of St Andrews, Fife, Scotland

1718 Robert Sandeman born in Perth, thirty-two miles from Edinburgh

1719 Rev John Glas is ordained Minister of Tealing, Dundee, Scotland

1721 Rev John Glas marries Catherine Black on 30 March

1722 First child, Catherine, born to Rev John and Catherine Glas

1725 George Glass born in Dundee

1728 Rev John Glas suspended from the Church of Scotland

1730 Rev John Glas deposed from the Church of Scotland

1730 Rev John Glas sets up the first Glasite church in Dundee, Scotland

1733 Rev John Glas erects small meeting house in Perth, joined by Robert Sandeman

1735 New Glasite church opened in Dunkeld, Scotland

1737 Rev Glas's daughter Catherine marries Robert Sandeman

1738 Rev John Glas returns to Dundee

1742 Handel's *Messiah* played for the first time at noon on 13 April, in Dublin

1745 Richard St Quinten born in Yorkshire in September

1749 Rev John Glas's wife, Catherine, dies aged forty-nine, from TB

1750 Many ports in Scotland involved in the whaling business

1754   George and Isobell Glass welcome a daughter to their family, named Catherine

1755   Population of Dundee reaches 12,400

1755   New Glasite church opened in Edinburgh

1759   George Glass visits London

1760   George and Isobell Glass arrive in London on 21 November

1762   *Earl of Sandwich* brig built in Yarmouth, 120 tons, crew of eight recommended

1762   Two boxes coarse baft/cloth shipped to George Glass in Senegal on 13 July

1764   George and Isobell Glass set sail for Senegal and Port Hillsborough

1764   *Earl of Sandwich* first listed in Lloyd's Register

1764   George Glass publishes his book on the history of the Canary Islands

1764   Board of Trade report on Glass's request for a twenty-one-year lease on Port Hillsborough on 26 June

1764   George Glass leaves Port Hillsborough with five crew members in longboat on 5 November

1764   George Glass writes from Tenerife prison to British Home Office on 15 December

1765   Captain T. Graves asks governor of the Canaries to release Glass on 22 March

1765   George Glass's ship attacked while anchored in Port Hillsborough in March

1765   George Glass released from Tenerife prison and reunited with his family in October

1765   *Earl of Sandwich* sets sail from Tenerife for London in November

1765   *Earl of Sandwich* arrives at Crookhaven in Cork on 21 November

1765   *Earl of Sandwich* departs Crookhaven on 26 November

1765   Glass family celebrate their daughter's eleventh birthday on board the *Earl of Sandwich* on 29 November

1765   George Glass and family murdered on board the *Earl of Sandwich* on 30 November

1765   Murderers anchor ten leagues from the shore of Waterford on 3 December

1765   Murderers row ashore and land in Wexford on 3 December

1765   Murderers arrive in Ross and hire four horses on 4 December

1765   Captain Honeywell of Newfoundland reports abandoned hull on 4 December

1765   Murderers arrive on horseback in Dublin on 6 December

1766   Murderers brought to trial in Dublin on 1 March

1766   Richard St Quinten confesses at Newgate Prison on 6 March

1766   Mutineers hung in the Stephen's Green area of Dublin on 7 March

1767   George Glass book 'The History of the Discovery and Conquest of the Canary Islands' printed in two volumes in Dublin by D. Chamberlaine in Dame Street and James Williams in Skinner Row

1767   Chamberlaine and Williams print 'A short Account of the Life of Capt Glas'

1771   Rev Robert Sandeman dies in Danbury in Connecticut

1773   Rev John Glas dies in Perth, Scotland, on 2 November

1777   Dundee Glasite church constructed beside St Andrew's Church on King Street

1890   Sandemanian Churches in America ceases to exist.

PART ONE
THE FAMILY

"An aim in life is the only fortune worth finding"
ROBERT LOUIS STEVENSON

1

Scotland's Glass Family

In the 18th century, the coastal cities of Dundee, Dublin and Dalkey, were all thriving in their own ways and were not greatly impacted by turmoil experienced elsewhere in the 1700s – at least not yet.

THE FATHER – Rev. Pastor John Glas (1695–1773)
"His character in the Churches of Christ is well known and will outlive all monumental inscription."

INSCRIPTION ON HIS GRAVE IN HOWFF CEMETERY
IN DUNDEE, SCOTLAND

Glasite Church, King Street, Dundee, Scotland

The Father: John Glas (1695–1773)

The life experiences of George Glass were extraordinary by any standards for the time. Life expectancy for men in the 1700s was only forty years in this part of the world. During the period in which he lived, his life's achievements would be difficult to equal.

It is easy to forget that the world was a very small place in the eighteenth century when it's population was just 700 million people, equal to half that of China today. Travel was also expensive and dangerous. Going beyond a short distance from home was not affordable or even safe for most. But George Glass saw the world as a place to be explored and there are very good reasons why he had a passion that motivated most of his actions almost from birth.

For our purposes and to avoid confusion, we will use the spelling "Glas" for George Glass's father and "Glass" for George and his siblings.

I first came across the name Glass, or "Glas" as it is often recorded, some twenty years ago while carrying out some local history research. George Glass was the son of the controversial but kindly scholar, Presbyterian minister Reverend John Glas, the divine, who was born, not in Dundee but in nearby Auchtermuchty, Fife, on October 5th, 1695. He in turn was the son of another church minister, the Rev. Alexander Glas of the parish of Auchtermuchty. Educated at Kinclaven and Perth Grammar School, John Glas later graduated from the University of St Andrews in 1713 and was licensed as a preacher by the established Presbyterian Church of Scotland in Dunkeld. In 1719 he was ordained as minister of the parish of Tealing, near Dundee, at the age of twenty-four. Two years later he married Catherine Black. Catherine was the eldest daughter of another Perth church minister. This family had very deep roots in religion. George's father, Reverend John Glas, quickly developed a devoted following and became renowned for his captivating but lengthy sermons, which sometimes lasted as long as four or five hours.

By all accounts John's marriage to Catherine was a very happy one but with some challenges along the way. The couple went on to have a total of fifteen children, which was not uncommon at the time. The reverend and his wife would have been regarded as pillars of society in Dundee and beyond. The happy family life continued and all was calm in the household till the Reverend John Glas suddenly caused some unexpected consternation. He publicly declared his strong belief that "there is no warrant in the New Testament for a national church and that National Covenants are without scriptural grounds and the true Reformation cannot be carried out by political and secular weapons but by the word and spirit of Christ only". In other words, the concept of the clear separation of Church and State is supported by the New Testament. This was one way to rattle the cage of the established and very conservative Presbyterian Church of Scotland.

While the reverend Glas was a prolific writer and had an established and devoted congregation, unfortunately, because of his public proclamation, he was suspended from his ministerial functions in 1728, stripped of his stipend and was finally deposed two years later in 1730 by the Church for expressing beliefs that were thought to be heretical at that time. For a man with a wife and fifteen children, losing that stipend would seem to be a disaster. However, supported by his own devout following, in what could be viewed by some as an act of revenge (although he does not appear to have been that type of person) he quickly established his own Glasite Church in Scotland. In this way, he was able to provide and continue the services expected by his loyal congregation without interruption.

John Glas contended that there was a need for far more Christian love and voluntary action, which he was unable to foster within the Presbyterian Church. Being deposed and without his guaranteed income does not seem to have dampened his spirits. He practised what he preached and continued to enjoy life with his wife and fifteen children.

In the year when he was deposed, Reverend John Glas set up a Glasite Church of Christ in Dundee in 1730, followed by another in Perth in 1733, historically the old capital city of Scotland. But the Glasites were not always welcomed. When the Reverend opened the Perth meeting house, a zealous member of the established Presbyterian Church of Scotland commented, "Why do they not rive [tear] him in pieces?"

Glasite Meeting House, Albany Lane, Edinburgh, Scotland

Another Glasite church followed in Edinburgh in 1755. The attractive, windowless Edinburgh building still survives today, beautifully preserved, and is located on the corner of Barony Street and Albany Lane, with a meeting hall, dining room and a kitchen. At the time of John Glas's death in 1773, there were more than thirty Glasite congregations in Scotland, Yorkshire, London and in the New England area on the east coast of America. Ironically, the Dundee church building is now a distinctive white-painted meeting hall for the Presbyterian Church of Scotland, located on the grounds of St Andrew's Church on King Street.

Dundee was expanding rapidly at this time. From 1750, the city's population more than doubled to 30,500 over the following seventy years. The fact that Reverend Glas was able to sustain his large family without an official income would suggest that some of his close supporters were both wealthy and generous, and this also reflected a healthy local economy. Establishing a church requires capital, and judging by the

Glasite Meeting House –
Top Hat Wall Pegs

quality of the Glasite buildings and their locations, money does not appear to have been an issue.

With so much changing in Dundee, Reverend John Glas stuck to his principles and continued both with his very lengthy sermons and with the expansion of his congregation. By today's standards, his methods were a bit unusual. To hold the attention of his flock during his long services, kale soup was served at intervals. As a result, locals often referred to his parishioners as those of the "kale kirk".

In the Glasite meeting house in Edinburgh on Barony Street, it is strangely unsettling today to see all those ground-floor windows blocked up. There is, however, a beautiful and intricate domed glass roof-light through which distracting passers-by can't be observed but which reminds the congregation where heaven is located! Members of the Church dressed formally for services. The many short spigots protruding from the walls on the upper floor in Barony Street are a reminder of the tall top hats, often silk covered, which were worn by men. These hats rested on the spigots when this was a busy meeting place. In the eighteenth century, there was even a collapsible version of the head wear, known as an opera hat. This helped the wearer to avoid blocking the view of others on the stage at the theatre or to fold it during a church service. Did attending those meeting house gatherings help to form the characters of George and his siblings in later life as the many sermons were explained to the congregation?

As breakaways, Glasites were strongly resented by some and actively discouraged from setting up meeting places when they arrived in Edinburgh. That element of persecution may have made an impact on young George, too, and influenced any ambitions he may have had to follow in his father's footsteps. It is likely also to have shown him that self-belief, confidence and a determination to stick to your principles are important in achieving personal goals in life. We don't know what impact it all had on his siblings but one brother decided to move away from the family and that is perhaps evidence of the strife some of them endured.

In 1739, at the age of forty-four, nine years after George's father was deposed, the General Assembly of the Church of Scotland removed the sentence of deposition against the Reverend John Glas, but there was a sting in the tail. He was restored as minister of the gospel of Christ but not as a minister of the Presbyterian Church of Scotland. A man of strong convictions, he still refused to renounce those principles that were deemed to be inconsistent with the constitution of the Church. Clearly, although renowned as a kind soul, John Glas was an unyielding man.

Following what at times was a traumatic and somewhat turbulent life, in 1730, he finally decided to settle in Dundee, where he spent most of his remaining forty-three years. This port on the east coast of Scotland was transformed during this time. The Glas family would have seen both the very positive advances in society and also the darker side that existed during such a major social transformation. Visiting slave ships, child labour in the factories, and the poverty of the nonskilled workers were clear for all to see. Much of the reverend's later years were spent somewhat alone as his wife passed away due to tuberculosis in 1749, when he was fifty-four years old, leaving him with the large family to care for. However, he survived for another twenty-four years and eventually died on 2 November 1773, at the ripe old age of seventy-eight, almost double the life expectancy of the period. He was finally laid to rest with his wife and predeceased children in Howff Cemetery in Dundee where his tombstone was erected with the help of prosperous donors four years after he died. This is just a ten-minute walk from the Glasite Meeting Place on King Street which still stands today.

One of Reverend John Glas's daughters was named Catherine after her mother. She married Robert Sandeman in 1737. Born in 1718 in Perth, Robert later also became a Scottish nonconformist minister. He had a far more adventurous life than Reverend John Glas and was very keen to expand the Glasite movement even beyond Scotland. Catherine's young brother George was just twelve at this time. He and his thirteen brothers and sisters must have been quite a spectacle at the couple's wedding. The strong influence of the reverend shows through, as his daughter's new husband, Robert Sandeman, also became a devout Glasite follower, and his sermons too were widely read by the Glasite congregations. In taking up the family challenge, Robert Sandeman became a Glasite proselytiser and brought Glas's new Christian sect not just south of the border to England, but in 1765 also across the Atlantic to Danbury in Connecticut, New England, where they became widely known as the Sandemanians. It would seem that the family liked to stamp their name on their own religion!

This was a momentous decade for many, when the Congress in America had proclaimed its independence. In the New England area, the Sandemanians were by now widely recognised for their almost extreme passivity in that time of turmoil. Going against the emerging values of the Industrial Revolution era in both America and Britain, they believed in strict adherence to the New Testament, declaring that the accumulation of wealth was "unscriptural and improper", a lesson repeated so often by his tutor, Reverend John Glas, in those long soup-nourished sermons. Following the successful expansion of his New England congregation, Robert Sandeman died in Danbury in New England in 1771, two years before the elderly Reverend John Glas passed away back in Dundee. In spite of all the stresses and challenges in his life, the obstinate reverend father figure outlived them all.

The Son: George Glass (1725–65)
Born in Dundee in 1725, just five years before his father was deposed by the Presbyterian Church of Scotland, what George Glass achieved in his short forty years on earth is, by any standards, quite extraordinary. As becomes evident, George was intent on squeezing every last drop out of his allotted time on earth. He now becomes the central character of our story.

Set against the family's strong and somewhat unconventional religious convictions and his father's courageous efforts to swim against the tide of the Established Church of Scotland, one might expect George to have been a man who took a narrow religious view of both his life and the world in

HMS Unicorn – 200 year old sailing frigate in Dundee

general. This was not in fact the case, and the reasons lie to some extent in what was happening in and around Dundee as George was growing up.

While Scotland's provost and magistrates declared that attendance at church was compulsory on the Sabbath, the exploding population and shortage of churches made that impossible. As many as 4,000 worshippers had to be turned away each weekend until new churches could be constructed.

Also, by the 1730s, when George was attending school, the British government feared that overdependence on imports of some essential goods was making the country vulnerable to foreign competition. Among the products at risk was whale oil. While many whale species were hunted, the most valued of all was the sperm whale. Its thin oil burned brightly and cleanly and was used in both household and street lighting. It was also prized as a high-quality lubricant in the quickly evolving area of spinning and linen manufacturing equipment. It was used extensively, too, for soap production. Still today visitors to Edinburgh can see some of the lovely hand-blown glass globes that originally contained and burned whale oil to light the streets. One can even be seen outside the old family home of Robert Louis Stevenson on Heriot Row.

Significant investments were made by entrepreneurs keen to share in the profits funding the expansion of Britain's whaling fleet. Dry docks were developed, where the new vessels could be built quickly and efficiently. Dundee and nearby Peterhead became the country's two major whaling ports. Dundee's whaling industry dates back to 3000 BC – the Bronze Age – so expansion came naturally. At one time more than 1,000 Dundee-built wooden ships of all kinds sailed the oceans of the world. Even today, the wooden hulls of an estimated forty Dundee whaling ships lie trapped beneath the thick ice of the Arctic, a region that attracted whalers from many parts of the world for generations. Dundee whalers even made their mark in South Africa, where the Scots developed a major whaling station near Robben Island. Partly as a result of over-hunting in both Antarctica and the Arctic, gradually these excesses made a serious impact on catch sizes and whale populations.

As a young man growing up in this environment, we can only guess how George's imagination must have been stretched and excited. A career at sea must have seemed a possibility, but with three generations of his family involved in the Church, such an ambition is unlikely to have been encouraged at home. This might have made him feel somewhat trapped. Escaping to a more exciting life would have been a natural thought for any young man who saw so much international travel and trade taking place on his doorstep.

The following appears in *The Newgate Calendar*, a popular publication of the day, giving details of crimes, trials and punishments of criminals, and gives a wonderful insight to George and his early education:

At a very early period, young Mr Glass afforded strong proof of an acute and penetrating understanding greatly beyond what could be reasonably expected at his tender years. After the fine genius of this promising youth had received some cultivation at a respectable grammar-school, he was removed to the University where he attained to a great proficiency in the sciences. Having taken up the degree of Master of Arts, he applied himself to the study of physic and surgery, in which he made a rapid progress.

As George was completing his university studies, Dundee was already one of Britain's significant shipbuilding ports. An industry that began with the construction of small wooden fishing boats grew to produce a whaling fleet and also general marine activity and ship construction along the docks. Apart from the many visiting whalers, the Dundee Whale Fishing Company, established in 1754, also had a permanent fleet of four large vessels of its own moored here. Repairs and maintenance were always an important element of the business. Over the years, explorers and whalers learned that these wooden hulls were much better able to absorb the pressures of Arctic ice than less flexible steel hulls, which could more easily be sliced open. As the Arctic was a prime whaling area, construction of wooden hulls became a thriving industry on the banks of Dundee's River Tay. Years later, it was here that the very last traditional three-masted wooden-hulled ship was built in the UK. This was the RRS *Discovery*, constructed for

Whale oil street lamp, Edinburgh, Scotland

Captain Scott for his ill-fated expedition to Antarctica in 1901–04. Irishmen Ernest Shackleton and Tom Crean were lucky to survive that particular adventure. As late as 1963, Scotland still operated a small number of whaling ships. For young George Glass, back in the 1700s, seeing all this hectic activity every day as he walked from school, and possibly university, down the hill to the port area would certainly have made an impact and fired his ambitions.

But shipbuilding was not the only thriving industry in Dundee at this time.

During the 18th century, the growth in the manufacture of linen was particularly strong in Ireland and Scotland. Dundee was the centre of Scotland's thriving linen industry. As whaling began its slow decline, the jute industry also took up the slack in keeping the local economy vibrant. Shipping created a huge demand for jute and hemp products. These materials were essential for the production of canvas, tarpaulins, sail cloth, sacking, webbing, ropes, clothing and much more. Hemp was the softer of the two materials but jute was perfect for what wooden ships needed most: high-quality canvas sails and strong ropes. Jute at one time was one of the world's most important and internationally traded materials. On the other side of the Atlantic, even the pioneers' horse-drawn wagons on the move across the vast prairies to the American West needed jute tarpaulins for cover and protection.

As young George Glass walked home each day in search of distractions from his studies, he must have been fascinated as he watched the raw jute being unloaded along Dundee's docks which came all the way from India and especially from the eastern region of what is Bangladesh today. The forest of tall masts and sheets of canvas along the docks, the colourful array of ships' flags from around the world, the orchestra of shrouds banging against the rigging in the easterly winds, the variety of nationalities and languages to be heard – all of this turned Dundee into a small but vibrant global hub. George is as unlikely as any others in the area to have been aware that locally processed jute was not allowed to be processed in the colony where it was grown. This ensured that most of the added value would be created for the investors back in Britain rather than in India. Dundee's jute imports peaked at over 200,000 tons per annum, an extraordinary volume for a relatively small city, and all imported on those ships that were unloaded in this little port on the River Tay. At its peak, there were over 50,000 people in the greater Dundee area employed in the jute industry and its offshoots. On seeing this activity on such an enormous scale, George would certainly have had serious ambitions to travel beyond both Dundee and his homeland and to experience whatever wonders awaited over the horizon.

Industry and commerce were central to almost everything at this time throughout Europe and elsewhere. Great wealth was being created for some in Dundee. New processes were being invented up and down the country. It was discovered that if the dry and dusty imported jute fibres were sprayed with a mixture of whale oil and water and left for some days, the fibres softened, greatly improving the manufacturing process and also extended the life of the ropes. Another bonus was that it was a lot easier on the hands of the rope-making workers who suffered from handling the rough material.

The rope manufacturing processes were also being revolutionised. Here again, Dundee became a leader. There were at one time sixty-one spinning looms for rope in the wider port area. When very long ropes were required, the automated production unit based on the spinning jenny simply spun the continuous length of rope yarn out the factory door and down adjacent streets till the required length was reached where it could then finally be cut. Just imagine all those open factory doors, the humming of the spinning machines and these long lengths of rope winding their way down the local streets! Some of these ropes were the thickness of an arm or more and the finished coils could weigh several tons. As young George Glass walked down Commercial Street and on to Castle Street towards the Dundee Docks to check out the latest arrivals from the other side of the world, he would have had to step over these enormous lengths of rope stretching along the streets, all waiting to reach their final length.

Every ship along Dundee Docks was secured to their capstans, those big revolving cylinders used for winding up these ropes. Every mast, sail and many anchors depended on them. Almost every street was buzzing with the sounds and full of smells and dust. Working conditions were often dreadful, and to keep production costs low, women and children were often employed and forced to suffer in the dusty factory buildings. This resulted in the spread of serious respiratory infections. For this reason, as time progressed, production was gradually shifted to India, once permitted, when local Dundee labour costs increased and the health issues were no longer acceptable in the motherland!

The wealth generated from whaling, shipbuilding, linen and the jute industries was enormous. Local trades were very well organised, grouped in to nine categories. Each had their own livery, banners and badges. These trades included weavers, tailors, shoemakers, glovemakers known as skinners, bakers, butchers known as fleshers, dyers, bonnet-makers and hammermen. The formal badges of the skilled citizens with trades can be seen clearly on tombstones today at the Howff Cemetery in Dundee. The family of the Reverend Glas benefited too, as more meeting rooms were needed in their churches for the expanding population and congregations as the Glasites spread their word from Dundee to Edinburgh to Perth and beyond.

Dundee's jute barons, such as the Baxter family and the Caird family, built beautiful villas in the area and later became involved in a wide variety of municipal works. Sir David Baxter also became a wealthy linen manufacturer and a police commissioner. He funded the Dundee Technical Institute, university foundations, Baxter Park and more. The Cairds pioneered the weaving of cloth, appropriately incorporating jute, and eventually employed over 2,000 people. While some like the Baxters and Cairds were responsible employers and made significant contributions to the benefit of the wider community, to a large extent, much of the wealth generated during this era did not trickle down. Dundee was not alone in this regard as this was the pattern throughout that period of the Industrial Revolution.

Living in the centre of Dundee, George Glass and his family were surrounded by these trappings of wealth. Like any young man, George would have been influenced by the excitement in the air and certainly would have found his family's Glasite way of life a bit restrictive, even though their lifestyle could have been described as relatively privileged for the time. Growing up with fourteen brothers and sisters, losing his mother when many of the children were still young and experiencing the disciplines of a strict religious upbringing must have made an impact on the young George. Certainly his father's strong belief that the accumulation of wealth was "unscriptural and improper" would have caused him to ponder. As we know, at times these beliefs made the family the focus of unwelcome attention in Dundee, Edinburgh, Perth and Galashiels where they had Glasite meeting rooms. As would be expected, George was immersed in his father's doctrine from birth and into his early teens, having spent many long hours in church. After all, attending church was actually the law of the land at this time.

The Glasite congregation was a very close-knit one. The members would have spent a great deal of time together during their weekly religious routines. Nobody would have been surprised if George opted to become a minister of the Church, just like his father, his grandfather, his wife's father and his brother-in-law. As he was born when his father was thirty-five years old, they are likely to have had a strong bond, unlike another brother who was so troublesome that he had to be "sent away". The obvious career path for George would have been to play an active part in the world of the Glasites and, perhaps, join forces with his brother-in-law, Robert Sandeman. However, as we know from the *The Newgate Calendar*: "Having taken up the degree of Master of Arts, he applied himself to the study of physic and surgery, in which he made a rapid progress." Already George was on a different track, and a career in the Church now looked highly unlikely.

In Dundee at that time, the qualification of surgeon was a highly respected one. Two hundred years earlier, the Company of Barbers and Surgeons was established. Members had to undergo a seven-year apprenticeship before sitting an examination held by the company's court of examiners. It was not until 1 July 1745, when George was just twenty years of age, that barbers and surgeons split and it was at this point that the Company of Surgeons was established. The name was later changed to the College of Surgeons. We have not been able to locate George's records in the Universities of Dundee, Edinburgh or Glasgow. Neither does he appear in the records of the Royal College of Surgeons. However, records of that period are not as comprehensive as they are today and he may even have served an apprenticeship to qualify as was also the practice during earlier times.

Clearly George was now very familiar with Dundee's extensive seafaring tradition. Seeing, almost every day, ships arriving from India, the Mediterranean, West Africa, the Americas and the Caribbean would have created an exotic picture in the young man's mind. It would also have been impossible for him not to be very aware that Dundee was recognised for its great industry in converting that shiny vegetable fibre imported from India into ropes of various kinds, essential for all sailing ships on the high seas. Dundee Port, for that time, was certainly an exotic sight, with single-masted cutters, two-masted brigs, three-masted barques and four-masted schooners, all dependent on locally made jute ropes, canvas sails and webbing. To add to this spectacle, the boat-building industry was booming right on George's doorstep. The visiting whalers must also have been quite a sight too, returning home from both the Arctic and Antarctica with their barrels of oil strapped together tightly on deck, ready to be used for street lighting throughout Scotland. All this international trading and shipping traffic covering the oceans of the world would have enticed any young man to want to be a part of it.

By now, his early religious discipline was beginning to fade as he became a young adult. His education so far had broadened his mind and taught him the basic skills of writing and research. We are not sure why he was attracted to the profession of surgery as there was no family history relating to this that is known, but that was the route he took to begin his career. In eighteenth-century medicine, surgery was seen by some as a last resort as a career since infection often killed the patient anyway. With barbers frequently carrying out surgical procedures in unhygienic surroundings, poor outcomes were common. Antiseptics did not arrive until 1867, a hundred years later. Anaesthesia only made its first appearance in 1846. Extraordinary as it might seem to us, this was the era of amputations without anaesthetics.

Armed with some surgical knowledge and a qualification, and having been exposed to the possibilities of seafaring from birth, George Glass quickly took to the sea to practice his trade. When he broke the news of his intentions to his father, the family would certainly have felt the loss, but in such a large household, it was probably taken in the right spirit, as there would be one less mouth to feed. *The Newgate Calendar* states:

> He afterwards engaged as a surgeon on board a trading vessel bound to the coast of Guinea; and in that capacity made several voyages to America. His superior qualifications gained him a distinguished place in the esteem of several capital merchants who trusted to him the command of a vessel in the Guinea trade; and his conduct proved highly to the advantage of his owners and equally honourable to himself.

Initially, George was hired by freelance merchants who were no doubt more than happy to have an educated and enthusiastic sailor and surgeon on board. Accidents at sea were frequent and his skills would have been in great demand. This was now a chance for him to acquire the seafaring skills needed to survive on board sail ships which were an essential part of trading between Europe, Africa, America and further afield. The next step in his career at sea was to join the Royal Navy and this was to open up for him a much wider view of the possibilities and opportunities which had attracted him to this life from the very start.

Joining the Royal Navy at that time may appear to have been the start of a glamorous career, but the truth was quite different. For the more fortunate ones, new volunteers like George Glass were first offered two months' payment in advance to entice them on board, a significant amount at that time. From this they were expected to buy their own bedding and hammock. Another significant benefit was that if they just happened to have personal financial problems, they were protected from creditors for debts due up to a value of £20 upon signing on. For some this meant they were spared a jail sentence or even transportation to the colonies. However, the other side of that coin was that an estimated 50 per cent of Royal Navy mariners were simply rounded up by agents of the Royal Navy who were permitted to pressgang young men into service against their will, as there was a huge demand for labour at sea at that time.

The activity of impressment was tolerated by the law. Below deck, sleeping quarters were cramped, ceiling heights were usually less than 5 ft and ventilation was poor. Dysentery and scurvy were common afflictions. In one study of thirty-three Royal Navy ships, almost 10 per cent of the crew had venereal disease. The tough survived and the weak didn't last very long.

London was still regarded as the primary port of the British Empire and by the 1750s, twenty eight percent of all British trade flowed through there. At the same time, Liverpool, Bristol, Newcastle and other coastal cities like Dundee, were also experiencing significant growth in both their populations and sea-going tonnage. In all cases, shipping attracted a host of trades and services to the port area. These often included anchor smiths, carpenters, coopers, keelmen (coal labourers), lumpers (loaders), pilots, lighter men, barge men, carters, sail makers, ship builders and more. A variety of merchants were also part of this diverse community providing the services of lawyers, agents, factors, insurance brokers and customs officials. However, one group of individuals always

Verdant Museum in Dundee displaying original rope making machines for ships which often required 20 miles of ropes for their rigging

tended to differentiate itself from this community and that was the mariners. They tended to live in distinct communities, close to the waterfront, and were both culturally and physically different. A London magistrate, Sir John Fielding, is quoted as saying "That their manner of living, speaking, acting, dressing and behaving, are so peculiar to themselves." For the young man, George Glass from Dundee, it is strange that this was the world which attracted him. His religious and conservative family upbringing would have been in great contrast to the company which he was now keeping. Some years later, writer and journalist, Daniel Defoe, stated that "they (mariners) are violent fellows and ought to be encouraged to go to sea". However, the *Tyne Trade Directory* of the period also described mariners as "a most robust, active, and fearless race of men, who, in time of war, supply the flower and strength of the British Navy" It appears that mariners while at work at sea were not seen as a threat to society but once back on land, following long periods of confinement in small and usually male environments on board ship, with time on their hands and money in their pockets, they were often regarded as a threat to the sensibilities of polite society.

George Glass's career at sea quickly progressed. As a midshipman in the Royal Navy, his skills and confidence increased greatly. Because of his conservative educational and family background, somewhat different from that social group described by Sir John Fielding, his rank in the Royal Navy was above that of cadet and this immediately gave him officer status and useful man-management experience right from the start. Navy disciplines were very strict and the various routines on board ship were often harshly enforced to maintain discipline at all times. These he would learn from and they would prove invaluable to him in later life. Sea service was indeed used as an alternative to a prison sentence as that discipline on board was respected as a corrective device for undesirables or an alternative to transportation to the colonies. Although still a young man, the strict discipline and the often very uncomfortable conditions which were part of everyday life at sea would have toughened up George Glass very quickly. At the worst of times, he might even have let his thoughts drift back to that windowless Glasite church in Dundee and those hot bowls of homemade kale soup.

Glass's early voyages were extensive. They took him south to Spain, to West Africa, to the Caribbean and even further south to Brazil and other parts of the Americas. However, it was the west coast of Africa which captivated him from the very start. Before long he even found time to sail up rivers flowing into the Atlantic from Africa's west coast and in particular to explore rivers in and around Western Sahara, Senegal and Guinea, most of which would have been uncharted and certainly very dangerous for visiting foreigners. In this region of the west African coastline, extensive sea traffic flowed north to Europe, south to Guinea and west to the Caribbean, Brazil and America.

George Glass was now a serious traveller by any standards, gaining invaluable experience at sea over an extensive area of the wider Atlantic and Mediterranean. To this point, it would be fair to guess that his conservative father and family back home in Dundee must have been very proud of his rapid career progression and seafaring adventures. How often he returned home to Dundee to share his stories, we don't know. However, although mail systems were slow but reliable, during his time as a naval officer, passing ships often exchanged mail bags with each other as they travelled in different directions, and George Glass would have been able to correspond with his family quite easily in that way.

Ambition was now about to propel George Glass into an even more challenging area of life at sea. This was to have a profound effect on the rest of both his personal and business career. Armed robbery at sea in one guise or another was part of a mariners experience in the 18th century. Staying on the right side of the law was the overriding challenge. George was about to be tested on both fronts.

2

Privateer to Prisoner of War

A privateer was a private warship. A shortcut to address the
high cost of funding the maritime defences of the colonising
nations was devised by the navies of England, the Dutch,
France, Spain and others. Known as privateering, this was a
very simple practice. Individuals, often businessmen, were
encouraged to fund, arm and fit out their own ships as trading
vessels but also as part-time ships of war. As their trading was
carried on as usual, buying, selling and even plundering
around the world became a way of life. However, these private
enterprise ships could also disrupt the trade of enemies,
conquer weaker communities, capture and trade slaves and

Dundee Ropes

bring home vast profits for themselves, their financial backers and their monarchs, if they survived. They were to all intents and purposes a back-up navy, which did not require the funding of monarchs or the public purse. All they needed was willing investors. and they were in no short supply as the returns could be enormous. While greed can make society poor, it can also be quite a motivator for some individuals.

Privateering as a way of life dates back to the time of Edward I, commonly known as Edward Longshanks (1239–1307), when he first granted, what were called, Commissions of Reprisal. These special awards permitted the holder to attack and plunder ships of other nations for profit without receiving any punishment at home. Profits were often shared with the Crown in order to obtain permission to prey on the enemy and carry out reprisals when deemed necessary. Later, in the 1500s, the business of privateering began to flourish even more when relations between Britain and Spain became hostile. One country's privateers were another country's pirates. Spanish galleons carrying gold, silver and spices back from America were often the target. Not only was privateer Francis Drake (1540–96) knighted for his circumnavigation of the globe, it is often forgotten that he was a very aggressive privateer and slave trader who preyed on Spanish ships for years as a pirate. As a result, he accumulated vast wealth and for fifteen years lived in luxury in the manor house known as Buckland Abbey, at Yelverton in Devon, which still stands today. Regarded by his own countrymen as a swashbuckling and titled hero, to his victims and their countries, he was regarded as a plundering pirate. This is a great example of the ambivalence of some governments of the time towards piracy. In general, the public's imagination was also captured by what was seen by some as a Robin Hood lifestyle of stealing from rich enemies for the benefit of others. Popular ballads of the day extolled the daring and glamorous deeds of those involved. However, all of this was to change in the 1600s.

While piracy was tolerated and even venerated by some, there was a line that even the pirates should not cross. This line was transgressed in September 1695, which just happened to be the year when George Glass's father was born. The transgression was so great that it almost destroyed one of the world's most successful businesses, the East India Company. It created political turmoil between Britain and India and transformed the somewhat acceptable Robin Hood image of piracy to one of a global scourge that knew no limits and had to be destroyed. It all centred around a man by the name of Henry Every. Born in 1659 in Devon in England, as with so many other privateers and pirates, he began his career in the British Royal Navy. After tiring of the Navy and its harsh daily routines, he was next employed by the governor of Bermuda and also established himself as a successful slave trader. In that sad trade, he had a major competitor known to all as the Royal Africa Company, an innocuous sounding name for a business that is reputed to have traded over 150,000 slaves of all ages, male and female. This was an English mercantile trading company, established in 1660 by City of London merchants.

Some years later, in the 1690s, a group of very wealthy individuals in London, headed by an English MP by the name of James Houblon, who had family connections with the East India Company, was in the process of setting up an expedition to salvage treasure from sunken Spanish galleons wrecked in the Caribbean. Established in 1600, the East India Company had become one of the greatest wealth creators of the day for investors in Britain. From 1657 on, it operated much like a multinational company does today. The largest part of its profits at this time came from trading cotton, calico and chintz, all sourced in India.

Houblon's Caribbean adventure was named the Spanish Expedition. The flotilla comprised four ships. The pride of the small but well-funded fleet was the frigate *Charles II*, a fast and well-armed vessel, with a total of forty-six guns. Considering that the firing of each gun required a team of six men, a total of 276 trained crew members were needed to man all the guns in battle.

On departure from London in 1694, spirits on board the *Charles II* vessel were high. Crew members were looking forward to earning anything up to the equivalent of ten

Privateers moored offshore

years' pay on this voyage from recovered sunken treasure and even the opportunity of a bit of pirating along the way. From London, they sailed south across the Bay of Biscay on the first uneventful leg of their voyage. As planned, they had their first routine stopover in the port of La Coruña in the north of Spain, near Santiago de Compostela, and planned to then catch the trade winds that would take them all the way to the West Indies. This is where the adventure went seriously wrong. A long delay in paying the crew while in port in La Coruña and an unexpected problem in obtaining the required sailing documents in Spain caused serious unrest on board. This unrest finally escalated to a mutiny, and the *Charles II* was seized by the unhappy crew. Mr Henry Every emerged as the elected captain. Seventeen mariners did not wish to take part in the mutiny and were amicably loaded into a longboat and sent ashore. Eighty remained. The *Charles II* was now in the hands of Captain Every. To conceal its identity, he immediately renamed her the *Fancy*.

Pirates of the day were surprisingly well organised and disciplined. They developed a range of clear and concise codes of conduct. The most sensitive one referred to how plundered treasure had to be distributed among the crew. In advance, each was allocated an agreed number of shares. Ordinary crew members might get one share, the ship's doctor one-and-a-half shares and the captain two shares. The captain was voted into his position by the crew and could also be removed at any time by a simple majority vote. Gambling was forbidden at sea and women were not allowed on board. Battle-wounded crew members were compensated in accordance with the severity of their injuries, with so much for the loss of an eye, so much for a leg, and so on. Majority rule was totally accepted.

All was designed to avoid quarrelling and discontent at sea and to create a level of justice, unity and harmony. Ironically, these codes or laws operated very well at sea and were outside the laws of nation states. They were in many ways much more advanced than those of most communities ashore. It was indeed a floating democracy and this underpinned much of their success over time.

Knowing that they might be followed, Captain Every and the *Fancy* immediately headed south for the Straits of Gibraltar and along the west coast of Morocco. In the 1600s, this was a very dangerous area. Apart from the East India Company fleet, few ships from Europe went south of the Equator. Accurate maps for navigation were scarce. In fact, mariners rarely continued further south than Guinea or the Cape Verd islands as they were known in the 1700s. With their impressive speed and heavy armaments, Captain Every and his crew overpowered three ships in the area, thus making the *Fancy* not just a stolen vessel but also guilty of piracy. This is where Every made a critical and life-changing decision. He abandoned what his crew thought was his plan to turn west from the Cape Verd islands for the Caribbean and instead continued south, around South Africa's Cape of Good Hope and then east towards Madagascar and the Indian Ocean. Word of rich pickings available from attacking Indian ships operating in the Red Sea had reached far and wide. Every was clearly aware of this. He and his crew next decided to alter the design of the *Fancy* in order to increase her speed, removing much of the upper-deck housing to reduce wind resistance. He hired additional crew at St. Augustine's Bay in Madagascar which was also a thriving slave trading base. Now the *Fancy* had become a very efficient war machine. By June of 1695, he had gathered other pirate ships, six in total, to give him a combined force of over 400 men.

At this same time, at the town of Surat, north of Bombay, on India's west coast, another remarkable voyage was coming to an end. This Surat city area just happened to be the regional base of England's East India Company with its enormous and very impressive castellated coastal fortress. Granted exclusive trading rights by India's Universe Conqueror Aurangzeb, one of the world's wealthiest men, for British interests, this was a vital trading post. One of Aurangzeb's largest ships and proudest possessions, the *Gunsway*, was returning home to Surat after the annual Hajj pilgrimage to Mecca, the holiest city for Muslims. Capable of carrying over 1,000 passengers, on this occasion, these included members of a royal family, Mughal princesses, many of whom were relatives of Aurangzeb. It also contained one of the largest treasures ever carried at sea, estimated to be worth US$20 million today. Critically, without his support, the East India Company in Surat, could not operate in India. Improbable as it might seem, this ship was the ambitious target that pirate Henry Every planned to attack. To even consider such a target was outrageous. It appears that he had kept this secret from his crew and patiently bided his time for almost a year as he waited for this opportunity.

With its altered design, the *Fancy* could easily outrun the bigger *Gunsway*. Catching up with it was no problem. Once close by, a few very lucky blasts from the *Fancy*'s cannons caused havoc on the target vessel. The element of surprise got Every and his men quickly on board. A bloody battle on deck followed and many of the *Gunsway*'s crew members were slaughtered. The pilgrims returning from Mecca were not prepared for this. Victory by the pirates was quick. Even they

must have been astounded at the amount of treasure stored on
board the *Gunsway*. If they had just settled for this enormous
haul, they might have simply been regarded as pirates who got
lucky.

However, Every's crew, having risked everything and waited
for so long for this moment, lost total control and went berserk
on board. What followed was shocking by any standards. Worst
of all, they raped and abused many of the defenceless Muslim
women passengers and tortured members of the crew in their
efforts to locate the treasures onboard. Some of the women
jumped overboard to escape from the violence and shame of
being molested. For this to happen to the pilgrims on their way
home from the Hajj pilgrimage was even worse. To do this to
members of the family of the Mughal Aurangzeb was to shock
the world, and it was most certainly overstepping the line of
tolerated pirate conduct and behaviour.

These actions initiated what was probably one of the
first global manhunts, and all on board the *Fancy* were now
the targets. Because of their ship's speed, Every and his crew
succeeded in gaining enormous distance from the crime scene
before the authorities in Surat, the Mughal Conqueror and
the East India Company could even consider giving chase. As
the perpetrators were mostly English, Aurangzeb immediately
blamed the East India Company for complicity, raided their
large seaside fortress, imprisoned all their staff and cut off
their highly lucrative trading rights. This had a devastating
impact on the both the local community and, potentially, the
British economy. News of the atrocity by British pirates quickly
reached the headquarters of the East India Company back
in London. Parliament was outraged at the prospect of the
profits of the Company being cut off. An order to capture the

pirates was issued by King William III and a substantial reward offered for the apprehension of Every and his crew, either dead or alive. Even other pirates were encouraged to capture the crew of the *Fancy* and share in the reward.

As the reports of the crimes and the formulation of search arrangements all took considerable time to complete, by now Every and his crew had a ten-month lead. Initially they headed to the island of Réunion, just north of the Seychelles, and to hide their identity, they posed as slave traders. To support this cover, while moored here, they bought ninety slaves. Additional hands were also needed to fill the gaps on board after some of the crew opted to remain behind in Réunion with their share of the loot. Guessing correctly that there might already be a price on his head, Every now quickly sailed south and back around the Cape of Good Hope, across the Atlantic and headed straight for Nassau in the Bahamas. On arrival, Every and his crew paid a substantial bribe to the governor of Nassau in exchange for a safe haven while they planned their next move. Here, they could rest in peace and secrecy for the moment. Part of this bribe involved donating the *Fancy* to the governor.

Next, Every and twenty of his remaining crew purchased a smaller vessel and headed back across the Atlantic, this time to Ireland. Still without being spotted, they landed safely in County Donegal on the north coast and pulled in to Sheephaven Bay on the Rosguill Peninsula, a shallow but well-protected inlet. Once rested again, they made their way on to Dublin, 170 miles south-east of Sheephaven Bay, from where they hoped to catch a ferry back to England. Despite the many bounty hunters now chasing the very well-publicised and generous rewards, it appears that the crew did make it to Dublin and also back across the Irish Sea to England. Unfortunately for them, their luck finally ran out and they were quickly tracked down in Newcastle, Liverpool and in various other parts of England and all transported to London where they would be tried together. This looked like the end of this extraordinary story, but somehow one pirate escaped capture and that was Captain Henry Every himself. How he got separated from the other members of his crew during that journey from Donegal to Dublin, we will never know. One of the most notorious pirates of all time was never to be seen again and vanished without trace.

Following two show trials in London and much publicity, the five members of the crew were all sentenced to death. On 25 November 1696, they were brought to Execution Dock in Wapping on the banks of the river Thames, which for over 400 years was a designated place for executions. Their nooses were deliberately made shorter than usual so that they would slowly choke to death when the hangman pulled open the trapdoor. To emphasise the seriousness of the crime of piracy, their bodies were not removed from the gallows for some time. While pirate and privateer Sir Francis Drake was revered in England as a hero, one hundred years later, pirate Henry Every upset the commercial world so much that he was instrumental in changing forever the global attitude to the crime of piracy.

And so, as we entered the 1700s, thanks to the plundering, torture, rape and crimes carried out by Captain Henry Every and his crew in the Indian Ocean, piracy was now officially regarded as a scourge, and severe punishments were imposed on any who dared to carry out this activity. George Glass and most mariners would have been very much aware of the history and the seriousness of this crime.

Against this background of piracy and its place on the high seas, in the seventeenth and eighteenth centuries, the construction of an efficient and effective naval battle fleet was a highly expensive, risky and time-consuming process. Monarchs often drained the national coffers in their desperate attempts to control the high seas with their fleets. In 1599 Queen Elizabeth I sent Robert Devereux, the Second Earl of Essex, to Ireland with 20,000 foot soldiers and 5,000 horses by ship, "to subdue this restless island once and for all", funding that excursion would have cost a vast fortune.

Control of the main trading routes was still essential to the colonising powers of the day. British fleets developed a considerable speed advantage over its competing neighbours in Spain, France, Holland, Portugal and elsewhere. According to a study carried out by Irish economists, Morgan Kelly and Cormac Ó'Gráda, between 1750 and 1850, boat speeds were increased by as much as 50 per cent. When rounding the Cape of Good Hope on South Africa's Atlantic coast and quickly escaping those treacherous seas and the enemy, speed was a huge advantage. This benefit grew out of the Industrial Revolution, which was gathering momentum as George was entering his thirties. Those countries depending on their powerful trading fleets and navies and who came late to industrialisation suffered badly by falling behind in the technology of the day. Replacing wooden parts with iron parts on ships gave them the ability to cope with much greater sail loadings from high winds, thus increasing both speed and safety. Hammering thin copper plating, secured with copper nails, onto the surface of the wooden hulls reduced rotting but also significantly reduced drag, which in turn delivered additional speed. Copper salts in the covering copper sheets had the great benefit of slowing down the growth of fungi, the cause of rot to ships' hulls, and prolonged the life of the vessels. These features created significant sailing advantages for British fleets. Having a ready supply of Dundee jute ropes and sail materials added to these advantages. As Britain exported a wide range of goods to their colonies, including manufactured goods, textiles, furniture and luxuries, speed was a great advantage over the competing colonisers, and also when trying to outrun pirate ships. Britain imported iron, gold, pepper, furs, whale oil, tobacco, cloves, sugar, camphor oil and much more. Here again, speed was vital to reduce costs and to avoid weather hazards and enemy ships.

Sadly, slave-trading too, was still a booming global naval activity. Bristol was one of Britain's leading slaving ports. The Royal African Company monopolised the enormous and very profitable British transatlantic slave trade. Led by the Duke of York, City of London merchants focused their brutal kidnapping efforts along Africa's west coast. The duke was the brother of Charles II, and later succeeded him as King James II. During a period when Edward Colston, a renowned philanthropist born in Bristol in 1636, and for many years ironically named the "father of the city", was involved with the company, a total of 84,500 individuals were coerced onto slave ships from West Africa to be sold on for forced labour to owners of the sugar cane plantations of the Caribbean. In Joseph Hawkin's 1795 book, *A History of a Voyage to the Coast of Africa*, he describes how when slaves were captured in West Africa, "poles where driven into the ground in rows, four feet apart, a loose wicker bandage round the neck of each, connected him to the pole, and the arms being pinioned by a bandage affixed behind and above the elbows, that they had sufficient room to feed but not to lose themselves or commit any violence." It appears that once sufficient numbers were rounded up on land on this occasion, they were then transported to waiting ships and secured in irons below deck and set sail for America. On this occasion, 500 men were captured. Hawkins also describes how at sea, "a violent inflammation and swelling of the eyes and eyelids took hold and this infected both those below deck and all the crew."

Between 1698 and 1807, to fully understand the enormous scale of this trade, it must be remembered that approximately 2,100 slave ships left Bristol for Africa. These ships could carry as many as 600 slaves on one voyage. In total it is estimated that 3.4 million Africans were forced onto British ships during that transatlantic slave-trading era. The imposing bronze statue of the philanthropist, merchant and slave trader Edward Colston which was erected in Bristol on Broad Quay in November 1895 was torn down and thrown into Bristol Harbour in June 2020 during the global Black Lives Matter protests that followed the police killing of George Floyd, an African American man, in Minneapolis. Today, as the savagery of slavery is more widely recognised and understood, the legitimacy of statues of others who profited from this occupation is being reconsidered in a new and better informed light. Even the monument of Christopher Columbus at the Spanish Arch in Galway in Ireland, which was presented to the city in 1992 by his home city of Genoa to commemorate the five-hundredth anniversary of his historic voyage to the New World is now viewed by some as venerating a pioneer of global colonialism.

Competition on the high seas was vicious. Only the strong survived in the long-term. George Glass was very much part of this seafaring world. To prosper, the trading routes had to be protected at all costs to continue the creation of wealth in the mother countries and to satisfy the demands of both monarchs and investors. Sourcing materials, building ships, recruiting, arming the vessels and training crews, were also both risky and a major drain on national resources. By 1799 the British Royal Navy had 646 ships in its fleet. This included 268 captured from the French. At the 1805 Battle of Trafalgar, Admiral Nelson had twenty-seven ships in his fleet alone, plus six support vessels, manned by 17,282 men. The French and Spanish had thirty-three warships and lost twenty-two of them. The Spanish Armada contained 130 ships, with 2,500 guns, and lost sixty of those, many of them off the west coast of Ireland. All this gives us some insight to the enormous cost to these countries.

From what he had witnessed, officer George Glass was very attracted to the opportunities provided by privateering. He certainly had by now acquired most of the key elements needed: naval skills, man-management expertise, knowledge of how to both attack and defend a ship and navigate in lesser-known areas of Europe, Africa, the Americas and the Caribbean. He also developed his language abilities and this proved vital later. Although still a young man, even by today's standards, his range of valuable skills made him a much-sought-after individual. As we recall and as is recorded in *The Newgate Calendar*: "At a very early period, young Mr Glass afforded strong proof of an acute and penetrating understanding greatly beyond what could be reasonably expected at his tender years."

While not yet a wealthy man, in 1746 at twenty-one years of age, George Glass had already accumulated some capital. He married his wife Isobell Hill in 1750 in the Parish of St Ninians. His career now took a new turn. When war was declared by England against France in 1756, and George's daughter, another Catherine in the extended family, was just two years old, he was determined to provide a good life for his wife and his young family. He concluded that it was now time to apply his accumulated skills and knowledge to the world of entrepreneurship. Not surprisingly, because of his range of talents, he easily succeeded in securing backers for the finance required to equip his very own privateer vessel. Ready to start the building of his fortune in this new role as owner and skipper, he again sailed to Guinea, and thus began his lifelong connection with this area of West Africa. This early adventure proved to be very valuable for both himself and his backers. His reputation had now moved up another rung of the seafaring ladder. While the practice of privateering was certainly still encouraged by many monarchs and investors of the day, it was a far tougher and more dangerous existence than generally appreciated, often involving violence, bloodshed and death. George would have known this only too well, but that would have added to his excitement and encouraged him even more. Having inherited his father's fierce determination against all odds, he was already a very focused individual.

For his next adventure, he invested a considerable amount of his own increasing capital. He hired his crew, loaded up his vessel with provisions and, watching the sails pick up the breezes of the English Channel, he headed south-west for Spain. Following only three days at sea, a mutiny broke out on board. Yes, he was very young to have acquired his own vessel, to command a crew of hardened seamen and to be the skipper in charge of all around him. Afterall, these mariners came from a very different world than his and violence was a way of life for them. To some he might even have looked like an easy target for a mutiny. And so his first cruel lesson at sea was about to threaten his ambitions in a way in which he might not have anticipated. For this to happen so early in his career could have been a shattering experience.

Described later with great understatement as "a disagreeable circumstance", a disturbance broke out on board while young Captain Glass worked below deck on his charts. When word reached Glass, he immediately arrived on the scene and, armed with his sword, "dared to single combat any man who would presume to dispute his authority". This came as quite a surprise to his sea-hardened crew, and following some moments of tense consideration, his challenge was declined. His crew backed down. Single combat with a sword was not what they expected. The captain did not stop there. He assured all that in exchange for the discipline he demanded, he would do all in his power to repay their loyalty. As mentioned, a single successful venture with a privateer at that time could reward

Marine ropes on board ship in Dundee, Scotland

a crew member with as much as ten years' wages. Their only fear was that they could also be classified as pirates and hanged if captured by their enemies. This young and well-educated professional man from Dundee was not an easy target after all. A tall man, who had more naval experience than any of his crew could have known, had impressed them so much with his courage, tough-mindedness and fierce attitude that he quickly won over all on board. While England fully supported privateers, his actions could now be seen by his enemies as a clear step in the direction of piracy. He had clearly progressed from merchant seaman to naval officer, to privateer, and now to the world of piracy.

Within just ten days of his departure from England, Glass came upon a richly laden French ship. With his crew now greatly encouraged by the outcome of the earlier "disagreeable circumstance", he and his privateers took on the French vessel. Moving from privateer to pirate was really not a big step! Following some fierce fighting, they overpowered their victims and took the considerable riches which were on board. From there they continued on across the Atlantic to the West Indies, where they unloaded their spoils. All crew members on board, including the skipper, were now a lot wealthier than when they departed from England just a few weeks earlier, and in true pirate spirit the booty was divided fairly between all. Most left much of their newfound wealth in safe keeping before heading back across the Atlantic to see what further spoils were available on the high seas. Were they pirates or privateers? That really depended on who they offended.

Little is recorded of the deaths and destruction wrought in this period of his privateering excursions, but Glass was now a hardened sea captain. He had seen and experienced it all.

He was set firmly on a path that had superseded his earlier passion for surgery. His ambitions were far greater and his self-confidence was at an all-time high. Master of his own ship, skipper of a tough and loyal crew, he was well able to repay his backers in London and look forward to a comfortable life ashore at a time of his own choosing. However, as was almost normal for those involved in privateering, following a period of great success and the accumulation of some considerable wealth, his luck changed. That high level of confidence was just a bit too high.

Feeling invincible, George Glass next engaged with a much bigger French frigate, square rigged on all three masts and often used for patrolling shipping lanes. Having sized it up from a distance, knowing how he could overpower all on board, he positioned his ship as best he could to overwhelm the French and seize whatever was stored below deck. These frigates were serious war machines and sometimes carried between thirty and forty guns. Following some cat-and-mouse tactics, Glass somehow succeeded in out-manoeuvring the large frigate. Using his hard-earned naval skills, he then roped his vessel to theirs. For over two hours, Glass's ship and the French frigate crew fought a fierce battle in hand-to-hand combat. This prevented the French frigate from firing its canons. The scene was certainly a bloody one. Injuries on both sides would have been shocking, with dead bodies, blood, and severed limbs strewn on the decks of the vessels. Glass was shot and badly wounded in the shoulder but he managed to survive the injury after he was quickly bandaged to stem the flow of blood. His surgical knowledge would certainly have helped in this emergency and knowing that a main artery was not damaged and that he could fight on.

Then, just when he and his crew were at the point of overpowering the enemy ship, a second French vessel arrived on the scene. Glass's crew now had a major challenge on their hands. They could have cut loose and tried to outrun the new arrivals but they decided to fight on. His crew knew him well at this stage and were loyal enough to back him. Perhaps they could even take both ships! With the second French ship joining the frigate and hacking away at Glass's crew, more lives were lost on both sides. Glass refused to strike his flag till the very end. Eventually, he and those of his crew who survived the bloodshed were forced to surrender to the French. Tragically, half of Glass's crew were slaughtered in this skirmish. He had also lost his prized possession, his ship. With his badly wounded shoulder, he was now a prisoner of war and would pay the price for causing so much death and destruction to the French. He could easily have been classified as a pirate, and the penalty for that was hanging. Was this to be the end of the road for George?

At a time when France and England were fierce enemies, Glass was imprisoned in Guadeloupe, a French island in the southern Caribbean and which was never colonised by the Spanish. While incarcerated there, with serious injuries from the skirmish and with little likelihood of receiving medical attention, the harsh treatment he received took a serious toll on his health. He lost much of his body weight, was treated as an enemy throughout and could easily have perished as he lay in irons. If he was not a tall, strong and healthy young man to begin with, he would probably not have survived.

Relationships between Guadeloupe, the Spanish, the French and Britain had always been troubled. All were more than familiar with Guadeloupe, visited by Christopher

Columbus in 1493. It certainly was not a place of welcome for
George Glass. His French captors could easily have hanged
him, but world politics intervened. Following one long and
gruelling year in chains during which he almost starved to
death, George was released when peace was declared between
England and France in 1749 and prisoners were exchanged
as part of the truce. Miraculously, he then walked, or perhaps
limped, free.

It is hard to believe that he was still just twenty-four
years old. If nothing else George Glass was a survivor, but his
privateering experience came at a high personal cost. His
father was still active and healthy back in Dundee and most
likely totally unaware of how his son's career had changed so
dramatically. George's mother died from tuberculosis just as
he was gaining his freedom in Guadeloupe, so he could not
attend her funeral in Dundee. How different George's life
now was as he struggled to recover from battle wounds, bad
health and financial loss in the sweltering Caribbean sun.

George finally regained his health and, believe it or not,
again contacted his financial backers, explained his wish to
carry on as before and quickly purchased and manned another
ship, before heading straight back to sea. His ability to do this
demonstrates the enormous attraction that profit was to his
backers and also shows how fearless and determined George
was. The potential financial returns were enough to make this
unending cycle of gain and loss an acceptable routine.

Although he survived the next skirmish, George again
lost his new ship and yet again was confined to prison. Lest
anyone forget, privateering, especially in this region of the
Atlantic and Caribbean, was a very precarious business. Staying
alive was certainly the biggest challenge of all, and George

Glass was good at that. Well-organised pirates, such as Captain Henry Every a century earlier, chased their prey and acted in packs. Wars raged in the Caribbean and Atlantic. Plunder and mutiny were almost a game, and only the fittest survived. George was imprisoned no less than seven times during this turbulent period of his life. We can barely imagine what new skills all of this bloody experience must have given him. That his health did not deteriorate beyond repair is also a miracle, as conditions in prisons in those days were dire.

At this time, pirates had now realised that if they created enough terror among their victims, they were less likely to hide their riches on board for fear of being tortured. With newsprint still in its infancy, the demand for sensational stories of atrocities at sea was enormous. This the pirates fully understood and often repeated shocking stories in order to increase the level of fear surrounding them and also to gain even further publicity. One example involved the British pirate Edward Low. Born in 1690 in London, by the age of thirty-four, when he died in Martinique in the Caribbean, he had built up a well-publicised reputation for terror and cruelty and was feared by all innocent passengers and crews on the high seas. Once when a targeted sea captain was overpowered during an attack, he threw a bag of gold coins overboard to frustrate Edward Low. In retaliation, he was quickly grabbed by his attackers and the furious pirate cut off the unfortunate man's lips, boiled them in his presence and then forced the captured victim to eat them.

Half a century later, George Glass had somehow succeeded in amassing considerable wealth in spite of his own trials and tribulations in the world of privateers and pirates. To suggest that he was by now a fully hardened mariner would be an understatement. Above all, he was a survivor in a somewhat cruel world.

In 1759, almost ten years after his near-death experience in the Guadalupe prison, George made his way back to London. At this time, the demand for individuals with his skills was at its peak. He was now widely regarded as a person who could make others very rich. His knowledge of the Canaries, West Africa and even the east coast of Brazil was far better than most at the time. Nobody doubted his ability to fight to the death to defend his property or that of his backers. Even humble butchers, bakers and candlestick makers were only too willing to invest in ships that could deliver enormous profits for their shareholders. Coffee houses, taverns, barber shops and almost any meeting place were full of people, both male and female, who were more than keen to buy a share in the next voyage. While success was not guaranteed, there were now enough stories and visible examples of individuals made wealthy by men such as George Glass. Many British stately homes of today are the result of these profits and the risks taken at sea by the likes of George. No doubt this was why he always appeared to be able to replace lost ships, crews and equipment and prepare once again for the next privateering adventure. All he had to do was stay alive.

George again returned to London to seek out new backers. However, on this occasion he intended to launch an exploration expedition rather than to plunder enemy ships. He had had his fill of privateering or piracy for the moment and also had accumulated a considerable amount of wealth. He could afford to relax, at least for a while. In preparing for the next possible adventure, he delighted in bringing his wife, Isobell, with him on a visit to London to enjoy some time together, meet some of his financial backers and share in some entertainment. Following his extraordinary challenges at sea and his long periods away from home, it was clearly a time when he and his wife could at last enjoy each other's company. Isobell would have greatly welcomed the visit to the city as she and her husband entertained possible investors and financial backers so that he could soon set about equipping yet another ship. London was booming, with a growing population of over 700,000. The city was teeming with ale houses, coffee houses, theatres, exhibitions and much more.

The new British Museum had just opened and the Covent Garden area was thriving with visitors from all over Europe and beyond. It was a time of hooped skirts, elaborate bonnets, top hats and dress coats, for those who could afford such luxuries. This was in the reign of George III, and while poverty was rife and parts of the city were very dirty, polluted, dangerous and overcrowded, the wealthy enjoyed extravagant lives of comfort and lived in beautiful mansions in exclusive neighbourhoods. For Isobell, sharing this level of comfort and extravagance with her husband would have been an eye-opener. While Dundee was a prosperous city on a small scale, this would all have been a totally new experience for her.

In London at this time, the anti-slavery debate was gathering momentum, even though slavery was not abolished there for almost another seventy-five years. However, its possible demise was already leading some investors to search for more acceptable investments, and George was a person who could provide these. He desperately wanted to get back to sea again where he was most comfortable. If George shared his ambitions with his wife, Isobell, we don't know as he certainly was away from his family and home for considerable periods. He may even have wished to take revenge on those who imprisoned and tortured him so badly in Guadeloupe but that is unlikely. Certainly, his lifelong ambition to be a significant explorer was still not satisfied. He still wanted to follow his own special secret ambitions farther afield. For better or for worse, on this occasion, fate intervened. In 1763 peace broke out on the high seas again and the destruction, mayhem and profiteering by privateers and pirates alike along the trading routes, was curtailed. And so, once Glass had repaid any outstanding debts to his investors, he decided to take some rest and to enjoy a little rare time with his wife and nine year-old daughter.

Europe, too, was entering a more peaceful era. The year 1763 saw the end of the Seven Years' War, a global battle between the great powers of the day, which had split Europe in two, with Great Britain on one side and much of the rest of the world on the other. The Treaty of Paris was eventually signed and this brought peace between Britain and its enemies in France and Spain. At last the risks of trading on the high seas were greatly reduced, and as a result international trade boomed.

Strangely enough, three years later, at the age of thirty-eight, with few other commitments and with time on his hands, in some contrast to his privateering life and recent experiences, George Glass headed for Tenerife in the Canaries, which by now was very well known to him. This port was a place where he could relax and enjoy the sunshine and some of the wealth he had accumulated. At that time, the Canaries were perfectly placed on the vital shipping route from western Europe and the major trading powers to the Americas. Privateers, pirates and slave traders all rubbed shoulders together here. Crews from all over the world were hired and fired and casually moved from ship to ship. Even here, popular opinion held mariners in very low esteem. While respected for their work at sea, on shore they were often feared. Canary Islanders were also well used to living with pirates, slave traders and merchants coming and going from Europe and Africa. While most were welcome, memories linger. When the Berbers landed here in the early 1600s, with over 3,000 men and thirty-six ships, they captured 900 slaves and pillaged anything of value. They almost succeeded in destroying life entirely on the islands, but as George Glass relaxed in the warm sunshine, all was now calm in Tenerife.

Similar to Dalkey Island, the Canaries also have their own small offshore island at the most northerly point, all part of the Chinijo Archipelago. The little volcanic island of La Graciosa, a bit bigger than Dalkey Island, lies within view of the north of the bigger island of Lanzarote. The straits between Lanzarote and La Graciosa were renowned for attacks by pirates and were routinely patrolled in the 1760s by Admiral Edward Hawke – who played a major role in bringing an end to the Seven Years' War – and his two heavily armed galleons. The island was uninhabited and only local fishermen usually came ashore. With little water or vegetation, it was an arid and desolate place and might appear to be of little interest to those passing by. It is no surprise, however, that others saw it as an excellent hiding place with its coves, rocky coastline and safe beaches. Spanish treasure ships frequently sailed off its shore as pirates lay in wait, hoping for some easy pickings, unless Admiral Hawke happened to be on patrol. Christopher Columbus and Walter Raleigh both enjoyed themselves in the Canaries at one time or another.

From La Graciosa's tallest peak, Las Agudas, approaching victims could be spotted miles away. While waiting there for passing merchants and slavers, often moored at Playa de las Conchas, if given half a chance the pirates would attempt to take all on board, including valuable slaves. Legend has it that in the 1760s, a British ship, fully laden with the spoils of war and resting at anchor at one of La Graciosa's many hidden sandy coves, was cornered by a pirate ship. Seeing the approaching danger, the British ship's crew had barely enough time to hide their treasure before they were overpowered, tortured and then slaughtered. That booty was never found and entered the long list of lost treasure.

The Spanish Crown was so concerned by this ongoing threat to their passing ships that they constructed solid fortresses on several of the islands to discourage the pirates and support their own fleets. They also became useful as prisons as George Glass was to discover to his cost later. This cat-and-mouse game between pirates and the naval ships of Britain and Spain and France and Portugal was alive and well when George Glass now took up his peaceful residence. We can only imagine what the atmosphere must have been like as he was surrounded by the good, the bad and the ugly. Fortunately for him, he had money to spend, could now speak Spanish fluently and set about enjoying the more pleasant side to life on Tenerife in the 1760s. It is doubtful that he had Isobell with him on this occasion, as it was still too dangerous and also no place for their young daughter.

At this time, while the Canary Islands were an exotic meeting place for traders and crews from Holland, Spain, France, England and far beyond, the local population was poor. The few eminent families which were here had each adopted their own particular saint who was honoured every year in a major festival where each family tried to outdo the other in extravagance. The narrow roads were paved with pebble stones with the men riding on horseback and the women on asses seated on a comfortable chair instead of a saddle. As the prevailing Atlantic trade winds made the islands a perfect resting place for those sailing from various parts of Europe to America, the Caribbean and Brazil, the local population profited from these passing strangers throughout the year. Imports from Ireland at this time included beef, pork, butter, candles and salt-herrings. The gatherings of course also included many pirates. Notorious individuals from the Barbary Coast, Spain, Portugal and elsewhere brought vast fortunes here for safety. One of these, revered in the Canaries, was a man by the name of Ivan Rodriguez Felipe. By the year 1727, his large fortune included no less than sixty properties throughout these islands. Francis Drake, Christopher Columbus and others would also have sipped Malmsey wine in the sunshine here as they passed through.

The Canaries were home to another unsavoury activity of which George Glass was very much aware and of which his earlier religious upbringing would have made him conscious. In spite of growing pressures to shut down the trade, Tenerife was where the slave ships arrived in great numbers from West Africa before they headed across to the Caribbean, back to Bristol and Liverpool in England, or even up to his own home town of Dundee. Human trafficking has a long and savage history in this region. Even the past rulers of Lanzarote carried out raids for generations in North Africa to capture Moors, Berbers, Fulani and other African slaves in order to trade them on for profit to passing vessels.

In total contrast to the typical mariner's lifestyle, during this break from his seafaring career, George found time to successfully translate the manuscript of a Franciscan monk from Andalusia by the name of Juan de Abréu de Galindo, a sixteenth-century historian. This academic endeavour was followed by George's 1764 publication entitled *The History of the Discovery and Conquest of the Canary Islands*. The manuscript of Juan de Abréu de Galindo formed the basis of this book. Glass points out that "Tenerife is the centre of the trade to Europe and the British colonies in America" and as a frequent visitor, it is easy to understand why he enjoyed his time here so much. He also pointed out that "the greatest part of the aforesaid trade to Europe and the English colonies is in the hands of the Irish Roman Catholic merchants settled in Tenerife, Canaria, and Palma". It is likely that English was widely spoken at that time although he was fluent in Spanish. Very significantly, Glass also states: "I warn all strangers to these islands, to observe the Alegranza, Lancerota, and Fuertaventura are, in almost all our maps and sea charts, placed twenty-five or thirty miles too far to the southward, for the true position of Alegranza is about the latitude of twenty-nine degrees thirty minutes north" Clearly he was aware that the sea charts generally available were not accurate and this played a significant part in our story later. By all accounts, George's translation was very well received. Not only did it cover the history of the Canary Islands but also their more modern early history. To the semi-illiterate barefooted crews of the ships moored along the docks where George was relaxing, this talent of his made him a very unusual mariner.

It is hard to believe that, after achieving so much, George Glass was now just thirty-nine years of age. His history book certainly confirmed his academic credentials and wide knowledge of not just the Canary Islands but also the surrounding geography and its evolution.

Once again, it is well to remind ourselves that all of Glass's entrepreneurial efforts and the rewards he had now accumulated were in stark contrast to his earlier Presbyterian life in Dundee and even more in contrast with his father's strict Glasite Church beliefs. One wonders how he reconciled his thoughts at night when at home alone with Isobell and

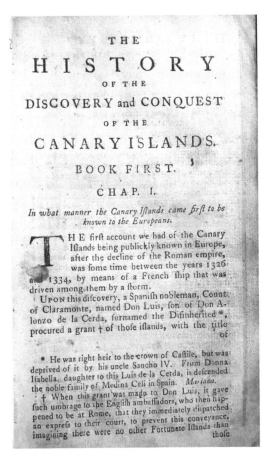

THE

HISTORY

OF THE

DISCOVERY and CONQUEST

OF THE

CANARY ISLANDS.

BOOK FIRST.

CHAP. I.

In what manner the Canary Iflands came firft to be known to the Europeans.

THE firft account we had of the Canary Iflands being publickly known in Europe, after the decline of the Roman empire, was fome time between the years 1326 and 1334, by means of a French fhip that was driven among them by a ftorm.

UPON this difcovery, a Spanifh nobleman, Count of Claramonte, named Don Luis, fon of Don A-lonzo de la Cerda, furnamed the Difinherited *, procured a grant † of thofe iflands, with the title of

* He was right heir to the crown of Caftile, but was deprived of it by his uncle Sancho IV. From Donna Ifabella, daughter to this Luis de la Cerda, is defcended the noble family of Medina Celi in Spain. *Mariana.*
† When this grant was made to Don Luis, it gave fuch umbrage to the Englifh ambaffadors, who then hap-pened to be at Rome, that they immediately difpatched an exprefs to their court, to prevent this conveyance, imagining there were no other Fortunate Iflands than thofe

George Glas's leather bound book printed in Dublin in 1767

their young daughter with his experience of bloody battle, injuries, incarceration and death, and the huge financial rewards! Those very long sermons given by his father back in Dundee clearly were not as effective as the Reverend John Glas would have hoped! We don't know if he was aware of much of the details of his son's new life, although, while traveling, George did correspond with family members back in Scotland and with others. Perhaps, the reverend may have received second-hand accounts of the many dangerous sides to his son's adventures.

Having experienced the rewards, hardships and tragedies of privateering, suffering serious injuries, seeing half of his ship's crew slaughtered in naval skirmishes at one stage, and losing as many as seven ships on his travels around the West Indies, Brazil, West Africa and the Canary Islands, it was time for yet another new project for George. Reputed to have endured imprisonment no less than seven times, by coincidence, that was one imprisonment for every ship lost, we know that he was certainly not a man to fear challenges of any kind. His next adventure was indeed to be yet another extreme test of his character.

3

The Canaries Saga

Behind all of his adventures so far, George Glass's lifelong secret desire was to establish a deep water harbour or fort on Africa's Atlantic west coast or elsewhere in that general region, which he now knew so well. Such an establishment could guarantee him significant wealth and power. This was a serious ambition.

Eighteenth century map of West Africa - Cape Verd and Jalof territory

His hope was to build a major trading post, not unlike Surat on India's west coast, or even to establish a fortress and to use this as a base for further trading explorations. He must have reflected on the wealth-creators of his youth back in Dundee, the Baxter and Caird families. He was already very familiar with the coastline of Western Sahara, directly east and to the south of the Canaries, and he was especially interested in the Cape Verd, Senegal and Guinea regions, over a thousand miles below the Canaries. Senegal, with its long French colonial history, successfully traded groundnuts, cotton and fish. Not unlike today, fishing in that area was fiercely protected and highly valued, in particular by the Spanish. Cape Verd, six hundred miles west of Senegal, was discovered by the Portuguese in the fifteenth century, and its deep water harbour was especially important to them. When their galleons first arrived in the area, local tribes had never seen such large vessels before. Cape Verd and the surrounding area impressed Glass greatly and struck him as an example of what could be achieved once a secure deep water trading post and harbour were established.

Guinea, to the south, was renowned for its vast reserves of gold, iron and other minerals. It was still a very dangerous area, with hostile tribes and with very few reliable maps available for navigation. This also had development potential. Not long after he began his search of these western shores of Africa and surrounding areas to the south, Glass is thought to have made a surprisingly quick discovery of a deep, navigable river. It looked like he had hit the jackpot. Indeed, if viable, this would have totally changed both his life and his fortunes and might even have been the end of our story.

There is still today some considerable controversy about where exactly his famous mystery discovery was located. Glass went to extraordinary lengths to conceal its whereabouts. This was too great a find to have it stolen by others. Scholars and explorers have tested and debated the claim for over two centuries, and there are many different theories on where exactly it might be. Indeed, one could spend hours reading through many of the possibilities debated in several languages in *Memoria Digital de Canarias*, and online library established in 2002 and still end up none the wiser. Santa Cruz de Mar Pequena, Guedar, Reguela, Assaka and other locations along the coast of West Africa, have all been suggested at various times. The fact that George Glass is reputed to have made a "quick discovery" suggested to many that his discovery must have been close to the Canary Islands, perhaps just across the water on the coast of Western Sahara or even southern Morocco, or perhaps not. As these were all located along busy shipping routes, it's doubtful if such a discovery could have gone unnoticed for so long. As safe ports were of such enormous importance to mariners and to local tribes in the 1700s, surely others, and in particular the Spanish authorities, would not just have known of the location but would already have established a base of some sort there.

Having explored detailed maps of the region, read many reports, listed and examined the names of possibilities that emerge from time to time and searched for them, this is where I am going to go against the tide of opinion and point us to a different part of the west coast of Africa. I have good reasons for doing this!

Here is a confirmed fact that pointed me in this different direction: on 13 July 1762, we know that a consignment of two large boxes of baft, or rough cloth, were shipped from Amsterdam to a man by the name of George Glass at a location in Senegal. Somehow he had found a way to collect it there later. Clearly he was already familiar with the area. We also know that just two years later, George Glass again set sail for Senegal. In other words, it would be fair to assume that he was heading back to his earlier place of discovery. There are many possible locations on that very long coastline that might fit as a base from which to operate. In spite of extensive research by historians and scholars over the past two hundred years, the exact location of Port Hillsborough, as he named it, still remains a mystery. And now it is time to introduce a distinct possibility. I believe that he selected a location, not in an easy-to-discover location within a short distance from the Canaries but further south in the area of the Delta du Saloum, just beyond Dakar in Senegal. The coastal area, has myriad rivers flowing directly into the Atlantic, which would seem perfect for the construction of a fortified port. Deep rivers, easy access to the ocean and a convenient location on a busy trading route were all in place. The Cape Verd Islands, directly west of Dakar, were already an impressive trading base but not available to Glass, as the Portuguese had long before beaten him to it. The location of the Delta du Saloum is almost perfect and was not already occupied by the Spanish, Portuguese, French or British. The Spaniards did have a fort in that general area in the fifteenth and sixteenth centuries, and Glass was probably aware of that. The Portuguese also came to this area in the fifteenth century but they settled out on the Cape Verd Islands. Glass guarded very closely all the details of his "unknown navigable deep-river discovery". This secrecy is not surprising. At this stage, he would have been well aware that information of the exact location of his discovery could so easily be stolen by others. In those days, it was a clear case of finders keepers and this was usually accepted by the colonising nations.

Most indigenous people in this region were Muslim and the Jalof, also known as the Wolof ethnic group, was the largest of these. Arabic would have been spoken by many. The Jalof were greatly feared and were part of the slave-trading community working with the Portuguese for some time. The Jalof Empire dates back to 1350 and still played a very strong role in this region up to the late 1800s. They are recorded as the creators of "the first kingdom of Negroes" in the Senegal area. From contact over generations with Arabs and Azanhaji, they became "Mahometans" but later contact with Christians weakened that belief over the years. Glass's extensive local knowledge gathered during his time in the Royal Navy and from his personal exploits helped him to increase his focus on exactly where his long-term base should be. He certainly did not want to have it stolen from him having got so close to achieving his life's ambition.

Working quickly, once he completed his initial survey of the area that he believed would allow him to establish and own a major trading harbour or fortress, he immediately turned his ship around and once again headed north along the coast of West Africa, up the coast of Portugal, across the Bay of Biscay and straight back to London. He had now confidently named his discovery Port Hillsborough. While there is a place in the Grenadines named Hillsborough, the more cynical of us would say that Glass was being much cleverer than that. A man by the name of Wills Hill had the title of Earl of Hillsborough at that time, an Irish Peerage of the King George III era. It just happened that he was the president of the Board of Trade and Plantations in England (1763–5). As George headed back to

London with his drawings, measurements and outline plans, flattering the president of the Board of Trade and securing the attention of such an important decision-maker, whose full support was essential, would have been a wise move.

Once rested in London and with his confidence at an all-time high, armed with all his knowledge of Senegal, Glass cleverly negotiated a deal with the Commissioners of Trade and Plantations for his new Port Hillsborough discovery. This was a powerful and intimidating body whose influential twenty-man board once included the Archbishop of Canterbury. Undaunted by the power of the Board of Trade and being by now a very experienced trader, George began his negotiations with a demand for a thirty-year exclusive trading arrangement with the permission of the Crown. He probably knew that he was going to be forced to make some compromises and eventually succeeded in extracting a valuable twenty-year right-of-trading agreement for Port Hillsborough and which he had mapped out in such great detail. This agreement with the Commissioners of Trade and Plantations was a stroke of genius and shows us once again what a clever individual Glass was. It also guaranteed him the princely sum of £15,000 seed capital, a serious amount of money and worth as much as £3,000,000 today. Just imagine how he must have felt as he walked from the offices of Commissioners of Trade and Plantations, near the Houses of Parliament in London, with that signed and sealed document safe in his pocket. Sharing with Isobell the details of his coup would indeed have been a special moment for them both. There was, however, just one matter to be concluded before he could head for the bank. This planned creation of Port Hillsborough was all contingent on the strict condition that he somehow obtain an agreement of free cession of the mapped area from the local tribes for the Commissioners' final approval and that of the British Crown. Only then could he achieve what had been a burning ambition ever since he first went to sea. The Crown was well used to such agreements and also strongly favoured monopolies where Britain could exclude other nations from whatever products or resources were available in the acquired territory.

The Jalofs were very well established throughout this part of Senegal. They had been in the upper region of nearby Guinea for over 400 years. The powerful Mandingos to the south were restricted by the Gambia River and this gave the Jalofs easy and safe access directly to the Atlantic Ocean and Cape Verd. The Sanaga River to the north kept the Jalofs safe from the marshy Azagar region above. Arab Berbers also roamed through this region, trading in gold and slaves. A man of many talents, Glass, who had already proven his proficiency in Spanish, had also somehow found time to master Arabic. This area of West Africa was not well known to Europeans in the 1700s. His knowledge of Arabic would give him a welcome advantage in dealing with the Jalofs and any others when attempting to secure their agreement, as he must, in order to satisfy the Commissioners of Trade and Plantations back in London.

This man never gave up. All was now in place for his biggest ever challenge. Setting up another partnership yet again with a wealthy firm of merchants back in London, as before, they were attracted by Glass's honest reputation, plus the strong promise of ivory, gold, wood and spices and who knows whatever else. He was again ready to head out to sea on what could be the greatest voyage of his life.

In August 1764, with this new ship under his command, plus adequate funding to guarantee the success of this voyage, he was almost ready to set sail from Gravesend on the south bank of the Thames Estuary in Kent. His preparations for this journey were meticulous, as usual. As was typical of British ships of the day, this vessel would have had a very ornate stern section, with leaded windows, and these quarters were where Glass would spend much of the voyage. Some ships of that time even had painted false gun ports to discourage and deceive attackers. A typical routine before sailing, which must seem strange to today's mariners, was to seal all the portholes and hatches and set controlled fires of straw below deck to smoulder for several days in order to create an effective smoke chamber. This was quite effective in killing the cockroaches and rats which infested most ships in port and caused havoc with food supplies.

For some reason, on this challenging voyage of almost 2,000 miles, George decided to bring with him both his wife, Isobell, and their daughter who was now just ten years of age. For that period of life at sea, this was highly unusual. In fact, many sailors regarded it as unlucky to have women on board. Rather than it being bad luck, it was more likely that crew members might take a fancy to any woman during long journeys out at sea and neither the husband or wife would want to cause friction with the crew on board when strict discipline was essential at all times. It also says a great deal about Isobell. To cope with the very rough life of mariners at sea, their crude language and often unclean habits, she must have been more than capable. Captain Glass would certainly not have risked having her on board if he was not already very impressed by her abilities. Even in the time of pirate Henry Every, crew members were absolutely forbidden to bring females on board. It was also unusual that Glass chose to expose his wife and young daughter to the expected hardships of the journey ahead. In those days, living accommodation on these vessels was cramped, sometimes wet and certainly not comfortable. The limited diet on board, too, played havoc with health. George Glass's decision to bring his family with him indicated his belief that this really was going to be a safe and enjoyable voyage that all would enjoy and which would allow him to finally share his long held dream with his small family. A proud man, having his family with him at what could be viewed as a £3,000,000 moment is understandable. With no other close friends to share this experience with him, having his wife and daughter by his side would have added greatly to his sense of fulfilment and enjoyment of the anticipated achievement which lay ahead.

Isobell's husband had been away from her for a great part of their married life, and she was now about to experience something she could never have imagined in the past. She would also be given a real insight to her husband's career and share in seeing his dream come true. If all went well, and why would it not, it was likely to be his last major adventure before retirement and perhaps even basing his family in this exotic place. A life of riches, servants, sunshine and peace. What more could either of them ask for?

As the moment of departure neared, every member of the crew was involved in loading up general supplies and enough provisions for the journey. Ship's biscuits, known as hard tack and made from flour, water and salt, large quantities of ale and some wine, salt beef, pork, fish, cheese and some live chickens, were all hauled on board. Ale was generally used for hydration instead of water as it was less likely to become contaminated over long periods at sea. Because of the poor ventilation and in spite of the rodent smoking exercise, the scourge of rats and other vermin below deck made the preservation of food an enormous challenge. Avoiding sickness at sea was vital, as a serious illness often meant death. Scurvy, caused by a lack of vitamin C, could be a killer. Bleeding of the skin and joint pains were the early warning signs. On one British Naval expedition in the 1740s, from a total crew of 2,000, more than 1,300 men perished from scurvy. Their illness was described at the time as "luxuriancy of funguous flesh", in other words, swollen, spongy, bleeding of the mouth. It was only in 1747 that James Lind, a naval ship's surgeon from Edinburgh, first discovered that eating lemons and oranges cured this very painful affliction. Unfortunately, the British Navy did not publicise Lind's cure for another forty-two years. To this day, there is a fresh water well on Dalkey Island, close to the Muglins Rock in Dublin Bay, known to all as the Scurvy Well. Throughout the seventeenth and eighteenth centuries, its curative powers attracted many visiting mariners who drank from this to help prevent the dreaded scurvy while at sea.

Once Captain Glass finally gave the order to cast off and the bosun ensured that the enormous canvas sails were correctly unfurled, they slowly eased away from Gravesend Docks, just twenty-two miles downstream from the centre of London and twenty miles inland from the sea. Sailing down the River Thames, they passed Canvey Island and Southend-on-Sea, heading out past Margate and on into the English Channel. Filled with great anticipation and probably no small amount of anxiety, they waved goodbye to England for the moment. At this time all ships' officers had to maintain strict discipline on board to try to keep morale high, combat boredom and avoid mutiny, which was always a possibility. Captain George Glass would see to this.

On leaving the English Channel, Glass set a course leaving Calais on the horizon on their port side as they headed out the English Channel towards Plymouth. Now in the open sea, they turned south of the coast of Ireland and well below Crookhaven harbour in Cork on their starboard side. Continuing directly on to the north of France and across to the choppy Bay of Biscay, they made good progress. Clearing that notorious bay, even on board very large ships, can turn seasoned sailors green. The captain's wife and daughter remained below deck at this time as they adjusted to the pitch and roll of the ship's hull, hoping that their seasickness would soon disappear. Paying close attention to the trim and ballast, Glass was well aware that allowing the bow of his vessel to be pushed down into head waves in this area could so easily result in the breaking off of yardarms or even the shearing of a mast. If they came crashing down on deck, serious injury or even death would result. Repairs while at sea were usually not a problem but injuries of any kind attracted infection and this had to be avoided. Glass would have experienced this in his earlier days as a naval officer and privateer and would be wary. The other great danger in the unpredictable Bay of Biscay was being hit by a broadside wave. This can so easily cause a ship of any size to get smashed and rolled on its side, known as a Chinese gybe, or even to capsize. On the other hand, the skipper always has to avoid being "pooped", hit by a big stern wave, which could rip off the ship's rudder, making it impossible to steer. This is a very serious challenge when running downwind. Fortunately, at this stage, they had a headwind which was making progress slow and laborious and kept the crew busy as the bosun barked out his orders. Less obvious is the fact that all of these stresses on a typical pliable wooden hull constantly twist and stretch its oak planking. This in turn creates small leaks, and ships like Glass's would have established a regular routine for pumping out the bilges to prevent damage to the ship's provisions below or even sinking in extreme cases. So clearing the Bay of Biscay was always a big relief for both skipper and crew.

Following a restless night on board in the continuing choppy seas, Isobell Glass and her daughter rose early and looking very pale on deck, they both enjoyed the fresh air as they began to get their sea legs. Later that day as they had now past the Bay of Biscay, they headed on towards northern Spain and south beyond the port of La Coruña. At this time, the sea grew calmer and the air became considerably warmer. Their route took them down the long coast of Portugal and on past Lisbon. George Glass was in his element and very much relieved to see his wife and daughter on deck and beginning to enjoy the voyage for the first time. The crew too did their best to moderate their behaviour and language and even waved and smiled at the ten year-old child who was delighted with the friendly company. As George's wife and daughter were watched very closely by him, the crew already referred to Miss Catherine for the youngster and Mistress Glass for the captain's wife. With Gibraltar some distance away on their port side, the coast of North Africa was soon in sight. The air grew warmer again as they sailed past Tangier, Rabat, Casablanca and steadily on towards Villa Bens. While the shoeless crew had no problem in walking on the scorching hot deck planking, it was far too hot for Miss Catherine to play on. The crew kindly hauled up buckets of Atlantic seawater when she came on deck to cool it down and the child delighted in splashing the seawater at her mother and crew. All in all, this was a happy voyage and Captain Glass too was enjoying the daily more relaxed routines. At this point, to their far west, they could just about see the outline of the Canary Islands, a sight so very familiar to the child's father.

The captain didn't waste any time on board as the crew had now settled in to a dependable and safe routine. Once he set the course early each day and instructed his bosun on what compass settings to adhere to, he then went below deck each morning to put the finishing touches to some vital documentation, something for which he had a great skill having already earlier that year proven his ability to create well-ordered documents for his 1764 book *"The History of the Discovery and Conquest of the Canary Islands"*. This time he was in the process of committing the final details to paper for the design of his new port and its surroundings. He worked tirelessly on his maps, schedule of construction activities, layouts for his proposed settlement, materials and equipment lists for requisitioning, and also the more difficult drafting of legal documents which would be needed in the final submission of his claim to the Commissioners of Trade and Plantations back in London.

The days continued to pass quickly. The crew's routines set a regular pattern of activity for all each day. Isobell Glass had now almost become part of the crew and took more and more interest in her husband's map reading and course settings and clearly enjoyed the tasks. The vessel rocked reassuringly as it ploughed through the waves in the south-easterly headwinds, progress was steady and without serious incident.

Before he was required on deck for the more challenging sea conditions, within three weeks, Glass had completed a very impressive collection of documentation. These papers could change his life forever. He knew that this was likely to be the most serious test yet of his ability to put to paper a compelling and credible port development case, which would be scrutinised in the finest detail before reaching the floor of the House of Commons in Westminster. He desperately hoped that the Commissioners would eventually accept all of these documents in support of his claim before parliament and then for final approval by the king.

Back on deck again, Glass checked the ship's compass, scrutinised the very limited charts that were available for this region and which he knew to be inaccurate and unreliable, and described for the bosun the next landmark to watch for. In his recent book on the history of the Canary Islands, he had already made a critical observation which was now more important than ever given that he had his family on board – "In all our maps and charts of the coast of Barbary adjacent to the Canary Islands, the part of it situated between the latitude of twenty-nine degrees thirty-minutes, and twenty-seven degrees thirty minutes north, is falsely described, as may easily be perceived by the general map of the islands, and the African coast adjacent to them". He also stated: "I am certain many have been deceived, and thereby run their ships ashore at night". His years of experience at sea were of special value to all on board this particular voyage when setting their course over the coming days. The crew also paid special attention to the rigging and reset the sails as instructed by their captain, sensing that the more difficult part of their passage lay directly ahead. This next landmark was to be Cape Bojador in Morocco, at latitude 26.1333, located along a treacherous reef-lined stretch of coastline to the west of the Sahara. The Portuguese explorer Vasco da Gama sailed past here in the previous century on his historic journey of discovery to India, as did the East India Company fleets in the 1600s. By the middle 1700s, the East India Company had increased their voyages along this route and on to India to over fifteen each year. The Venetian slave trader, Alvise Cadamosto, also left fascinating descriptions of the various tribes that inhabited this coastline in the eighteenth century. On any basic sailing chart, even today, all seems quite innocent here in terms of navigation. However, on heading for their next mark of Cape Bojador, they now entered a serious danger zone. This threat was so dreaded that it prevented many earlier experienced explorers from venturing south beyond this point on the map. Many died here. Myths of marine monsters terrified mariners on reaching this part of the African coast. Over thirty shipwrecks were also recorded during the 1700s in the region. For centuries, ships were known to simply disappear in the area. The coastline is spectacular. Although it is relatively flat, it is dotted with massive red sand dunes that slope down all the way to meet the choppy sea. Further along, huge waves break over the fearsome reefs just below the surface which indicated a depth of less than six feet in places. Inexperienced mariners in the 1700s and earlier always thought it safest to hug the shoreline. However, in this area, that would be disastrous.

The very strong prevailing south-easterly winds made progress slow. On the other hand, further out to sea, flat calm waters in the doldrums with absolutely no wind, were also to be avoided. Becalmed mariners there had often perished from lack of drinking water when stuck in the wrong area. However, worst of all was the invisible and little known geology of the rocks along this coastline. Their strong ferrous composition played havoc with compass settings. That was a nightmare for navigators as they could no longer trust their readings and if they did, disaster was certain. It is no wonder that earlier explorers were terrified to travel further south. This is all where the experience of Captain George Glass was invaluable. He had explored this coastline for years, both in the Royal Navy and also as a privateer. Knowing exactly where to avoid along this coast made it a much safer voyage for him and his crew. It would also explain why it was still possible for him to find unexplored and uncharted territory here. Few would have the courage to do so. This was another unique talent of Glass.

While this region was beyond the reach of many in the 1700s, it was nevertheless of vital importance to Spain as a major fishing area. Whales, seals and a wide range of other fish species were in abundance. Many of these fishermen operated out of the Canary Islands to the north. They regarded this as their home territory, as did the Spanish authorities. Apart from the great fishing resources, on land, this area also had great potential for the extraction of gold, copper, iron ore and even diamonds.

In the stifling dusty Sahara winds coming from shore, when the sun was at its highest and almost directly above, Isobell Glass and her daughter would have done their very best to stay in what little shade was available on deck. Members of the crew would often erect temporary canvas awnings to create shaded areas and to prevent sunburn and attempt to stay cool in the blistering heat. Walking across the unbearably hot deck planking was even more of a test for the barefoot crew as they continued to sail south. Below deck too was stiflingly hot and far too claustrophobic for the young child. However, as the afternoons cooled down, they would have had great fun together watching the flying fish leaping from the waves to flop on deck. Capable of reaching heights of almost twenty feet, these little fish could just about make it over the ship's gunwales. Seeing dolphins riding the bow wave and perhaps the occasional pods of sperm whales, pilot whales or an occasional killer whale passing by would have added even more to the spectacle for the captain's wife and child to enjoy. The beautiful sunsets at the end of every day became even more spectacular as the warmth of the red evening skies rippled across the huge canvas sails. This evening spectacle also greatly encouraged mariners who believed that a "red sky at night was a sailors delight".

Captain George Glass would have been in his element, of course. For once he could enjoy the experience of seeing his family relaxing on deck with him when it was not too hot to do so. He would also have been much relieved to have passed safely through that very dangerous area running south from Cape Bojador to Cape Blanco, which was the halfway point from the position of the Canaries to their final destination. The gleaming-white rocky coastline rising from the east created a shelter onshore for when the strong westerly winds later came in from the Atlantic, blowing across the huge forest of acacia trees beyond. Known in this region as the gum forest, these trees thrived almost all the way down to Cape Verd and were a treasured resource for the tribes in this area. Their honey and gum were guarded closely by the local Gualata and Sanhaga peoples. From here, it was to be a straight run down to Cape Verd. Even though discipline on board was strict, for the crew too, for the most part this would have been a less stressful voyage than usual, with time to perform their many daily tasks at a more leisurely pace. They would often spend their off-duty time practising their knots, whittling wooden models of all kinds, playing musical instruments, singing shanties, recounting times of past voyages, playing cards and dice games and drawing. Some even carved toys for young Catherine to play with during their long uneventful days. All of this helped to reduce the stress and loneliness of life during the long voyage. The novelty of having females on board would surely have amused the crew, but Captain Glass always kept a sharp eye on everybody. To pass the time, his daughter also started to embroider a small napkin, or sampler as they were called at that time, and this, too, was a novel sight for the deckhands. Often using a range of vividly coloured silk threads on linen, these samplers were treasured and usually given as gifts in those days. Samplers were also a reflection of social class. Children of the wealthy had time to enjoy such gentle pastimes, whereas children of the poor had tough labouring jobs and very little free time of their own. The crew were well aware of the captain's reputation as a tough skipper, and in front of his wife and daughter, would be on their best behaviour at all times.

With air temperatures continuing to rise as they neared their destination, Glass's dream was finally within his grasp. As the sun set beyond the Cape Verd Islands on their starboard side, we can only guess what his thoughts might have been as Cape Verd itself on Africa's coast lay off to the port side. The volcanic Islands were discovered by the Portuguese in 1449. Not wanting to waste time, he kept to the port side and closer to the coast as he searched for landmarks that were familiar to him. When Charles Darwin passed through here on his Voyage of the Beagle and headed over to the Cape Verd Islands for exploration later in 1832, he described in detail their black volcanic-rock landscape, the remarkable cuttlefish and the kingfisher birds resting on the castor-oil plants. His notes also included details of the acacia tree, which is significant as its gum, highly valued in this region, will became important in our own story later. As the Voyage of the Beagle was a very well-funded scientific one, which carried a highly qualified crew of seventy-four, they had an enormous quantity of delicate scientific equipment on board. The heavy brown fine dust that blew in from the coast of Africa and covered their deck could have seriously damaged their many precision measuring devices. Glass and his crew would have seen this same dusty coating on their deck, and daily scrubbing was an additional chore till they passed this area. Surely, after all the hardships, time away from his family over the years, injuries, ship losses and even deaths at sea, happy days must now be just around the corner! Captain George Glass had earned his spurs. All that effort was about to be rewarded. He might even have considered bringing his elderly father down here at some point. Imagine how proud he must have felt at being able to show his young wife, who had a very protected life back in Dundee up to this point, this fascinating region of the Atlantic and the ever-changing coastline, sights and sounds of West Africa.

Once past the protruding headland of Dakar, it was a straight run down to the Delta du Saloum. At Cape Verd, the land had risen and, having followed miles of flat, featureless shoreline for some time, they had just rounded the highest point, approximately 400 miles south of Cape Verd on the mainland. This spectacular delta area extends over forty-five miles along the coastline and contains more than 200 islands and hidden inlets. This was an area where anybody could get lost but also an area of great potential for the captain. The bosun gave the commands for reducing some sail, and carried on by the now-gentle breezes, the ship left the choppy Atlantic Ocean behind for the first time in weeks, and sailed inland. They were likely enthralled by the giant mangroves and the clear water teeming with fish and shellfish below, a host of new sights and sounds surrounding them. This was what real exploration was all about! The sounds of the red-billed fire finches, terns, curlews, sandpipers, the flamingos and even the occasional grunting of buffalo and warthogs in the distance all would have been a fantastic surprise for Glass's wife and daughter and indeed for most on board. Whether or not they noticed the beady eyes of the watching crocodiles we can only guess.

Three rivers meet here in the delta, and to select a safe mooring location, Captain Glass carefully steered inshore towards a point already firmly etched in his memory, the place that he had already named Port Hillsborough. Was this really to be the end of the journey?

Once they located a safe mooring place, they dropped anchor. After lowering their huge canvas sails, tidying all the ropes and paraphernalia and clearing the working surfaces, they all set about preparing for a relaxing meal on deck as the sun set in lovely calm water for the first time in over two months. A change of clothes and perhaps even the use of a makeshift shower on deck for some, brought smiles to the faces of all, including the tired crew. Isobell Glass and her daughter, now dressed in fresh colourful clothes, were the centre of attention at their long folding table under the night sky as the plates of food, tankards of ale and some wine from the Canaries were consumed. Even young children were given weak ale in those days to avoid illness from drinking contaminated water. All on board must have thoroughly enjoyed this moment. Everybody was safe and in good health. They had arrived. Strange animal sounds created a magical atmosphere, with the deep mangrove swamps running to the water's edge hiding nature's curious eyes and clouds of mosquitos. It all took some time to get used to. Although very humid, thanks to the breezes coming in from the Atlantic the temperature was a pleasant 85°F, falling to 75°F as night approached, perfect for the exhausted crew and passengers. That first night was one to remember for all on board. Hopefully they also remembered to bring some mosquito nets.

As we know, this was by no means a holiday trip for George Glass. This was a well-funded and meticulously planned expedition. All his efforts would be worthless unless he could now get the local Jalof king to provide him with the vital cession signature required to secure their loyalty to Britain. He would then have to safely transport that signed document all the way back to London to claim his reward. He already had almost all of the necessary paperwork completed. The detailed plans were fully drawn up. Constructing his safe harbour and a fortified fort for trading, accommodation and control could come later. Glass wanted to immediately begin the negotiations with the Jalof. However, he knew very well that some patience would be required and that this might take time and not be as straight-forward as he might hope. He needed to be cautious as there was a great deal at stake.

Tribes in this region were aware that visiting Europeans were more often than not slave traders. They themselves also traded slaves taken from other local tribes with the Portuguese, passing Berbers and others. With a staggering 84,500 individuals, male and female, adults and children, kidnapped by the slavers over the years from this area of Africa alone, the total misery and loss caused by ships looking just like Glass's would have made him and his crew objects of fear and danger from the moment they were spotted off shore. Word would have travelled quickly down the coast. Slavers had not only destroyed the lives of individuals and families here for generations but also entire communities. George Glass would have seen the slave ships crammed with human misery on many occasions back home in Dundee and on his many visits to Tenerife, probably without giving them very much thought. Here at anchor, this was a different matter and he had to be careful, especially with his family on board. Many on shore in this area of the delta who would have been aware of the arrival of this ship would now be on high alert. Were these white visitors friends or enemies? Captain Glass also would have had no way of knowing that at that moment there happened to be a serious shortage of food in the area, almost at severe famine level. Suffering and desperation were widespread. Local tribes were fighting for their survival. The beautiful and seemingly very peaceful surroundings were very, very deceptive.

The Jalof tribe had ruled here since the 1300s. They were described by white traders as tall, very black, very hospitable, great talkers, fierce, great swimmers, courageous and never likely to back down in battle. They washed four to five times each day and so would have been far cleaner than any visiting Europeans. As reported at the time by the Venetian Alvise

Cadamosto, "They are as expert as any European can be in their own business." For George Glass and his crew, that was the good news. Conversely, other reports state that they were savages, extremely poor, liars and cheats. It seems that opinions in the 1700s could differ as much as they do today! They also traded slaves with Arabs, Azanhaji and Christians. Their most successful and powerful king was Zukholin. History tells us that the Jalof king was always selected by elders, and as long as he ruled well he remained in power. The king had as many as thirty wives who lived in separate groups of about ten in different villages. If a wife became pregnant during his occasional calls, she received no more visits. The king wore elaborate cotton shirts with wide sleeves, which were spun by the village women, but as their looms were very narrow, the final garment was made up of several panels stitched together, which made it all the more colourful. They also wore very wide baggy cotton pants. When gathered by a belt, all the excess material trailed behind on the ground just like a bride's veil.

Finally the time came to venture ashore. The next phase of the Port Hillsborough plan was about to begin. Whether they admitted it or not, tensions among those on board were probably now as high as among any hidden observers on land. Being a cautious and experienced privateer, Glass decided that the safest approach would be to send just one scout ashore to show that no threat was posed by them and that this was not a squad of slavers possibly set on killing their king and kidnapping men, women and children. One thing in their favour was the relatively small size of their vessel. Such smaller ships were sometimes known as guineamen. As so many natives had been kidnapped from this area, slave ships were often big enough to hold as many as 600 almost naked unfortunates packed tightly together below deck like sardines. Glass's smaller vessel did not look threatening and may have reduced the level of fear. On the other hand, the Jalofs did not have large ships of their own, even of this size, and instead used small zoppolies or canoes for transport. This strange vessel would have been viewed as something of great value.

No doubt the reward offered to that lone brave scout who agreed to row ashore by himself must have been attractive enough to make him climb down over the gunwales and into the longboat which they had lowered below for him. He was totally unarmed and totally apprehensive about how the local population might react to his arrival. On the face of it, the task was a simple one. The water was flat calm and the distance to the beach was short. All he needed to do was attract some attention, express friendship as best he could if he was greeted by anybody, try to set up a meeting with the local king and assure the locals that this was a peaceful mission. Sometimes, sign language is enough when a language isn't shared, and smiling always helps.

All on board now assembled along the gunwales to watch and enjoy this first contact with the local Jalof tribesmen, that is, if any appeared. George Glass lifted his telescope to his eye and scanned the mangroves along the deserted beach to search for any sign of activity. The unfamiliar sounds from the wildlife in the dense mangroves added to the excitement and apprehension. As soon as their scout rowed to a landing place and climbed out of the boat in the clear, warm and shallow water, he waded ashore, pulling the longboat behind him till its own weight secured it in the sand. He looked around as he nervously caught his breath. Nothing happened. Had they come ashore at the wrong place? He waited and waited and even looked back to see if his captain would call him back to the safety of the ship. For thirty minutes or so, still nothing happened.

Then Captain Glass sensed movement in the dense tropical growth just beyond his scout. Those on board were close enough to both see and hear what they thought might be the local welcome party as a shape eventually emerged from the shadows. From their anchor position close to the shore and in the silence which surrounded the crew, they would be just about able to hear some of details of any discussions or exchanges which might take place. So far, so good. As it turned out, the local welcome party comprised just one tall, impressive, and very black figure. The approaching Jalof warrior was naked apart from a slender piece of goat skin covering his privates. Worryingly, he was carrying his African danta hardwood shield on one arm and also had with him a Turkish-style scimitar. The dantas were used effectively in battle and often shown on ceremonial occasions. The scimitar was a different kettle of fish!

Captain Glass watched closely as his crew pressed forward in case they might miss something. They were certainly not prepared for what was about to take place. Their scout continued to walk nervously towards the approaching warrior, taking great care to keep his raised hands in the air and to show clearly that he posed absolutely no threat and was not armed. The young lad even began to wave cautiously and smile. His crew mates back on the ship followed each and every one of his footprints in the white sand as he made his way closer and closer to the meeting point.

Everything then happened so quickly. Few could be quite sure of exactly what triggered the scene that followed.

Shock often does this to us when faced with the unexpected. In the blink of an eye, to the total horror of all watching from the ship's safety, including the captain's wife and young daughter, the Jalof tribesman drew his razor-sharp scimitar from behind his danta shield, raised it high above his head and with just a few swipes, viscously slaughtered the scout in mere seconds. For a brief moment, the young lad's terrified final screams of agony echoed around the bay. A cloud of finches and terns immediately burst into the air in fright, causing all on deck to gasp out loud. The unfortunate young man's bloodied, lacerated and twitching body collapsed down on to the white sand. His bright-red blood turned the pristine beach into a shocking crime scene. Silently, and without any further gesture, the Jalof warrior retreated as calmly and as silently as he had arrived, back once again to the darkness of the mangroves. Apart from the eerie sounds of the tropical birds in the trees above, the silence was total. With absolutely no forewarning or provocation whatsoever, the dream of a lifetime appeared to be turning into a nightmare for Glass. All on board stared in silence and shock. The sight of the young man's dead body on the beach would now be etched into the minds of all on board forever. No one would ever forget his terrified screams or his final moments on earth. Few slept well that night.

It would have been all too easy to simply lift the ship's anchor, set the sails once again and try another approach, or even just to head for the safety of home. Glass was already a wealthy man from his privateering days. He and his family could live well without Port Hillsborough. He had little reason to risk his entire crew or to expose his sheltered wife and innocent ten-year-old daughter to any more horrifying sights.

But that was not the kind of man this Dundee skipper was. Never one to ever give up easily, Glass was not going to walk away from the ambitious plans which he had mapped out in such detail for his Port Hillsborough project. While the others might never have seen such a scene before, Glass had experienced bloodshed up close and even death many times. He knew only too well what real fear was. He had sacrificed far too much for this. And besides, there was the equivalent of £3,000,000 to be collected back in London at the offices of the Commissioners of Trade and Plantations for the financing of Port Hillsborough, if only he could finalise an agreement with the Jalof.

Following what must have been a very tense discussion with his wife, and indeed with all the crew, a difficult decision was finally made. It was also a very brave one considering what they had all just witnessed. They had come too far to turn back now, and a plan of action was agreed. The delta location was beautiful. The Port Hillsborough project looked viable and all they needed to obtain now was a signed document. Captain Glass even had all the very detailed documentation fully prepared.

Over the following days, it was agreed that once they had taken some rest, they would remain at anchor to clearly emphasise the seriousness of their intentions and not to be seen as visitors who were easily intimidated. Next they would send a fully prepared delegation ashore, there being more safety in numbers. They would also be visibly laden with gifts. This action should stand a better chance of success if the gods were on their side. If the worst came to the worst, they hoped to fight their way out of trouble on the beach and escape back to their ship. After all, there was not much difference between privateers and pirates and both knew only too well how to defend themselves.

Five selected members of the crew, including Captain George Glass himself, nervously climbed overboard and lowered themselves, one by one, into a second longboat and pushed off. Isobell Glass was no doubt terrified at what might happen as she watched them row the short distance to where the abandoned boat was still firmly held in the soft sand. At very least, they needed to retrieve the other longboat now resting beside the corpse which still lay in a pool of congealed blood on the white sand. The delegation must surely have been terrified as they approached the shore, watching for any movement in the mangroves. No doubt, they were well armed this time, but their weapons would have been well concealed from view to avoid provoking any more unnecessary bloodshed. For all they knew, they could be outnumbered very quickly by whatever eyes were already following their movements. They may also have been unaware that the Jalof were renowned for their use of their azagays, long iron-tipped spears which they used both for hunting and in warfare. At any moment, a shower of these could descend from the mangroves upon the sailors.

With very little delay on this occasion, a group of Jalof warriors emerged from the dark vegetation, fully equipped with azagays, scimitars and decorated danta skin shields. Was this to be a new slaughtering party? This time Glass saw the difference before any act of provocation was carried out by either side. In the lead was a tall man colourfully clad in his short-sleeved cotton shirt and baggy pants with its "veil" trailing in the sand behind. Yes, this time they were in the presence of the Jalof king. Glass immediately recognised that this was a positive sign and whispered to all to relax and smile! Thankfully, it was not a large group and Glass and his crew would have taken some consolation from that, as the numbers in each party were about equal. At least they were not outnumbered.

Concealing their fears, they approached the king and his entourage and the two groups were quickly face to face. After they sized each other up, and with both parties making what seemed to be friendly gestures, the tension began to dissipate. Captain Glass was a tall, elegant man and had intentionally dressed for the occasion by wearing his impressive formal brass buttoned blue knee length frock coat and his ceremonial sword – a good ploy. The chief was of equal height and his colourful attire indicated clearly that he was a respected leader. Although they had a somewhat nervous start, the temper of the locals had improved and, to the great relief of all, the gifts were presented and discussions with the Jalof king finally began.

The Jalof were no fools. They were experienced negotiators, and their slave trading days would have made them very wary and ruthless opponents when required. Once Glass knew that the Jalof were satisfied that the visitors were not slavers coming to round them all up, the gifts were moved aside, he exchanged some pleasantries in Arabic and then produced a selection of his drawings to show the king what he had in mind. Pointing to surrounding landmarks and making frequent references to his own drawings, it was not difficult to demonstrate what he hoped to create there. As soon as they felt that enough had been achieved for this first day of discussions, they all rose together and bowed respectfully to their hosts before returning to their beached longboat. They made a point of towing with them the other boat rowed ashore earlier by their unfortunate crew mate and brought his bloodied corpse back for a burial at sea.

Once back on board, Captain Glass was clearly elated. Isobell was still shaken from the earlier slaughter but at the same time she was greatly relieved to have her husband safely back on deck. She knew only too well that he would never back down on this. At least they had broken the tension with the Jalof, opened the lines of communication and all were still alive. This was something her husband could build on. His grasp of Arabic made an enormous difference and he believed that he could now develop his relationships here.

Glass and his team continued the routine. Over the following days, they rowed ashore at agreed times and showed more and more of the well-prepared documents and drawings to the king. Drawings often tell much more than the spoken word. Eventually, after much explaining and pointing, a treaty was drawn up, the geographical area required for the development was defined and agreed, and finally the king signed this precious document. The nominated territory was at last ceded by agreement in exchange for the protection of King George III and the British forces, if needed. This would have given the Jalof king a distinct advantage over neighbouring tribes and would further strengthen his position with the local elders. As slave traders themselves, they knew that dealing with the British would also help their broader interests. No doubt there were other attractive promises made to seal the deal. George Glass must have been ecstatic. His long-term ambitions for his Port Hillsborough project were now so close to becoming a reality.

With the Jalof king's signature on the document, the celebrations began back on board that night. The rum casks were opened and this great achievement helped everyone to recover somewhat from witnessing the shocking slaughter of their young lad just a few days earlier. Now it was time to focus on practical matters as the extra slow journey from England and the additional time required to complete negotiations with the Jalof king had taken much longer than originally anticipated.

Although very happy with his achievements so far, things were not going quite as smoothly as Glass had first envisaged. The clock was ticking. The valuable signed cessation agreement was of course in his possession and now locked safely away in the captain's quarters, but he needed to get these documents back to the Commissioners of Trade and Plantations in London, a very long way from Delta du Saloum in Senegal on Africa's west coast. This should have been a time to mark the beginning of the creation of "Port Hillsborough", but there was just too much still to be done.

The senior members of the crew realised that, unfortunately, the unforeseen delays had run down their food supplies. Also, Glass's intuition told him not to fully trust those on the other side of the agreement. He had heard reports suggesting that the Jalof were liars and cheats and was still somewhat wary. The discussions and tragic experience on shore had left him with a deep feeling of unease. With his sixth sense and past privateering experience, for some reason, he felt that there was real danger in the air. As they finished their evening meal on board, just as a precaution, Glass instructed all to be on their guard and immediately posted armed crew members on deck to keep watch.

While still at anchor close to shore, a list of what was urgently required to feed and water everyone on board was drawn up. The following day, one of the longboats was again launched in the hope that they could buy provisions from their new "friends". Unfortunately for them, the near-famine conditions in the general area of the Delta had created grave food shortages. As a result, securing their provisions was far more difficult than anticipated. The cost of the supplies needed was also greater than expected. All of this added greatly to Captain Glass's general unease.

When the longboat crew eventually returned safely with the supplies and everything was hauled up on deck, the captain himself took charge of the unpacking with greater caution than usual. As it turned out, this was just as well. His suspicions were well founded. He quickly discovered that the fresh meat purchased on shore had in fact been poisoned. This came as a great shock as the securing of the Jalof king's signature suggested that they all wished to cooperate with the Port Hillsborough plan. In spite of the progress made, they now felt seriously threatened. That recent bond of trust with the Jalof had been broken.

Realising that he had to act quickly to avoid starvation at some stage and further risk to his young wife, ten year-old daughter and crew, Glass made another brave but perhaps unusual decision. This was to keep his ship at anchor at what was to be Port Hillsborough in order to support the signed cessation agreement and to emphasise clearly to all observers that he had long-term ambitions for the site. He was not going to show any sign of weakness or retreat. Having considered all his options, his next decision was that he and five men would launch one of the longboats and go elsewhere to purchase essential provisions. He also wanted to acquire a boat larger than their longboats to make local exploration safer. This would also allow him to carry more provisions back for his crew and perhaps also help with the local famine, which might further his cause. This plan was typical of the man.

Security on board was now a major priority, and a rota was agreed to keep watch around the clock. They did have some muskets and an ample supply of cutlasses, not unlike the scimitar carried by the Jalof, but they feared the Azagay spears, which could be used with great accuracy from a distance. The food that was safe to eat would be enough to keep the remaining crew and the Glass family well fed until his return. Here it must be highlighted that his decision to leave Isobell and his young daughter alone with members of his crew was unusual, to say the least. She must have been a very strong and confident woman to feel able to keep herself and her daughter safe without his help. Clearly, the experience which she gained on the voyage down to Delta du Saloum in Senegal had greatly impressed him and he must have felt confident enough to leave her in charge of his crew.

Taking some of their new supplies on board the longboat, which they had rigged with two short masts, they headed out to sea. While their sail area was modest and the longboat small by any standards, they could make good progress in the prevailing south-easterlies if conditions were favourable. Glass and the five men headed out of the Delta and turned starboard to the north. They soon past the Dakar headland once again and continued all the way up the coast of West Africa, past Cape Verd, Cape Blanco and Cape Bojador on the long and dangerous journey up to the Canaries. There were no obvious other stopping points for provisions along that flat and sandy coast, and as he also planned to buy a larger craft for exploration, he thought it best just to keep going, in spite of the distance. This was a challenging journey of over 1,100 miles for a relatively small, open longboat. Thankfully, although exhausted, they made it safely to the Canaries and finally sailed into the harbour at La Orotava at Santa Cruz de Tenerife.

Once Glass set foot on dry land in this busy port, as fortune would have it, he quickly spotted a ship about to set sail for England. He immediately arranged with the ship's captain for his recently signed and precious cessation treaty and all his supporting documentation to be transported back to an address in London, where it would then be delivered directly to the Commissioners to guarantee his significant rewards and to finally claim his Port Hillsborough territory. He could then repay his backers and start the greatest phase of his career. Now at last he could relax, get some rest and purchase food provisions, quantities of corn for the villagers back at the Port Hillsborough location plus a larger vessel for the journey back to Isobell and his other crew. Overlooked by Santa Cruz Prison, La Orotava port was a very busy and prosperous harbour. Everything he needed was available there, and from past visits, he knew exactly where to go and who to talk to. He could then load up everything in the new, larger vessel and immediately head back to Port Hillsborough to re-join his wife and daughter who were patiently and anxiously waiting for him.

Captain Glass's hard-won documents were now safely in transit to London, but he was in for yet another shock. Just a few days after his arrival in the Canaries, as he and his five crew members were resting and drawing up their provisions list in La Orotava, Glass was arrested by the Spanish authorities under the direction of Governor Don Domingo Bernardi Gomez

Rabelo. The official charge was "that Glas came to Alegranza, Lanzarote, from the coast of Africa without a pass, and was selling contraband". He was even accused of being a spy. His longboat and possessions were all immediately confiscated. On seeing how roughly their captain was manhandled during his arrest, in the interests of their own survival, his small group of terrified crew members quickly scattered and disappeared as fast as they could, which wasn't too difficult in such a busy transit port with sailors of all kinds and nationalities coming and going every day. Glass was dragged off to the prison in Santa Cruz de Tenerife to "be kept in irons, and denied the use of pens, ink, and paper". In the dungeon of this impregnable place, he must have felt totally desperate and even more concerned for his wife and child. Denied any way of communicating with the outside world, he now had no way of calling for help to fight the charges brought against him.

Over the coming months, as he lay in irons on a bed of straw, Glass could not have known that sometime after his signed cessation agreement and his maps, plans and drawings arrived safely back in London, events transpired which would have given him great hope, if he survived this ordeal. A certain merchant, Mr Anthony Bacon of the City of London, attended the Commissioners of Trade and Plantations on behalf of George Glass and presented to the House of Commons all the detailed documentation supporting Glass's claim. Glass would have been delighted to see evidence that a *Copy of the proposals of Mr George Glass, relative to an Harbour alleged to be discovered by him, and unknown to all other Europeans.* This was actually now on record in parliament. His extensive work during his recent voyage to the Delta was now the subject of very close examination. The very impressive collection of papers, according to the House of Commons record of the day, included the following:

> A copy of George Glass's Petition of the discovery of Port Hillsborough; his detailed Port proposals; a represent-ation from the Commissioners of Trade and Plantations to His Majesty dated May 15th 1764; a memorial including a scheme for opening trade between Europeans and the inhabitants; a representation from the Commissioners of Trade and Plantations to His Majesty upon Mr Glass's Memorial dated June 26th 1764; a copy of the instrument by which the Port of Hillsborough was ceded by the natives to Mr Glass together with an adjacent tract of

Santa Cruz Prison, Tenerife, Canary Islands, Spain

land, a copy of a translation of the instrument of cession, and a copy of a plan of Port Hillsborough.

These details are all contained in *Journals of the House of Commons, (ref: papers / Port of Regeala or Gueder)*. The considerable accuracy and clarity of his documents remind us of the extensive detail Glass had earlier provided in the writing of his successful book *The History of the Discovery and Conquest of the Canary Islands*. Here again his attention to detail and mastery of his subject tells us even more about his breath of talents.

For those with suspicious minds, there is another curious detail in the House of Commons records of later that day. This Mr Anthony Bacon who represented George Glass at the Commissioners of Trade and Plantations, was clearly a City of London friend of his. He also appears in the *Journals of the Board of Trade and Plantations*, Volume 12, 1764, just a little after all the Port Hillsborough documentation of George Glass was presented:

> Mr Bacon presented to the House, according to Order, a Bill for laying certain Duties upon Gum Seneca and Gum Arabic, imported into or exported from Great Britain and for confining the exportation of Gum Seneca from Africa to Great Britain only.

In other words, it was proposed that this valuable gum product could only be exported from Africa to Great Britain, thus giving the mother country a monopoly and the exclusive importer great financial advantage! The popularity of creating monopolies in favour of the motherland dates back to the previous century when the East India Company was at its trading peak. At this time, gum seneca and gum arabic were highly valued commodities and sourced in quantity from the general area where George Glass was seeking to build his Port Hillsborough project. Senegal gum and other similar gums were made from the solidified sap of the acacia tree. They provided important income for the Jalof and other tribes in the area and were highly prized. Arab countries have used the product for centuries as an emulsifier, for writing materials, and even in the making a sweetened ice cream-type dessert. Centuries ago, Egyptians also used it in the binding and preservation of mummies. Was George Glass aware of this as another wealth creator for his Port Hillsborough scheme? Perhaps this Mr Anthony Bacon, George Glass's friend, had been offered it as a "sweetener" for his own benefit to ensure that the Commissioners of Trade and Plantations would fully support Glass's request for exclusive trading rights? We may never know, but it is quite a remarkable coincidence that this second bill was not put forward within the documents of George Glass but by this Mr Anthony Bacon who is unlikely ever to have been to Senegal or even to have been aware of this valuable resource.

Fortunately, as the weekend approached, on Saturday, 15 December 1764, and probably with the promise of a bribe later, Glass succeeded in sending a written communication from his prison cell via a passing sailor. As luck would have it, this message would find its way back to the Lords of Trade in London. Some reports suggested that he concealed his note inside a loaf of bread to get it out of his cell; others, far more unlikely, stated that he scratched the details on a slate and threw it through the narrow window of his dungeon. Whatever method he used, it was enough to eventually have his situation addressed by the British authorities. Either way, he achieved his objective in spite of not being permitted access to writing materials. Despite the efforts of the local authorities, his call for help succeeded. In his message he described in some detail what had happened to him on his arrival in Tenerife and detailed his very harsh treatment and near starvation at the hands of the governor of the Canaries, Don Domingo Bernardi Gomez Rabelo. Somehow it appears the Spaniards had become aware of his ambitious plans for Port Hillsborough. Understandably, they feared that this could give England, both an old and recent enemy, a new stronghold in a very sensitive commercial area in the region, which could in turn threaten their extensive fishing grounds and perhaps even put their fortified base in the Canaries at risk. The Spaniards decided that this ambitious and troublesome Spanish-speaking foreign privateer was a serious threat to their general interests and should not be allowed to benefit from his new venture at their expense. Here is the Home Office report of his detainment:

> Among the home office records is a letter from Mr. George Glass, dated Tenerife, 15 Dec. 1764, in which he reports his seizure and close confinement in the castle. He suggests that the Spaniards dreaded interference with the important fishery carried on by natives of the Canary Isles on the African coast between Capes Bojador and Blanco, and asked for his release (*Calendar Home Office Papers, 1760–5*, par. 1631).

Three months later, another letter in Admiralty Records states:

> A letter to the secretary of the admiralty from Captain Thomas Graves, H.M.S. Edgar, off Senegal, dated 22 March 1765, states that opportunity was taken 'to enquire into the seizure and detention of Captain Glass by the

governor of Santa Cruz, Tenerife. The governor was
not very satisfactory in his reasons for imprisoning that
unfortunate poor man. It was then demanded to see him,
for he is shut up from ye sight of every one but his own
keepers, said to be kept in irons, and denied the use of
pens, ink, and paper; but this ye governor refused, and
would assign no reason why the poor man was kept under
such rigid confinement, even to barbarity, though pressed
to it in the strongest and most lively terms' (Admiralty
Records, Captains' Letters, G. 15).

Papers representing the case accompanied the letter, and with
it is another from Captain Boteler, HMS *Shannon*, which states
that the explanation finally given by the Spanish authorities
was that Glass came to Alegranza, Lanzarote, from the coast
of Africa without a pass, and was selling contraband (*Calendar
Home Office Papers, 1760–5*, p. 550).

It is interesting to see in these documents the mention
of the coastal area running from Cape Bojador down to
Cape Blanco in Western Sahara. Spain's sensitivity about
poachers operating into that region was understandable. For
centuries Spain had fished this area so intensively that some
species were already in decline. However, it still contained an
enormous quantity of fish, whales and seals, all of which were
located in the general region to the south of the Canaries.
Also, a large number of the Spanish fisherman working up
and down that coast of Africa were, for many generations,
based in the Canaries. Captain George Glass would certainly
have been viewed as a possible English spy or a poacher.
Gaining land rights in an area to the south of this strip of the
Western Sahara coastline was, for them, a step too far. Hence
the keeping of him in irons in a dungeon and the meting out

of rough treatment that might have ended with him dying and leaving little trace. He was to be taught a lesson and at the very least frightened off.

Over three months later, by 22 March 1765, the prisoner was still held captive in his cell in the castle and still denied the use of writing materials. Communicating for him remained nearly impossible, which was the intention, but as we know, he had already found ways to circumvent the strict rules. It would also appear that the Spanish authorities on the island were outraged by British intercession on his behalf, including communicating directly with King Carlos III of Spain. In an effort to discredit George's claims, it appears that the Island authorities forged documentation to "prove" that he did not actually have a legal entitlement to the area claimed as Port Hillsborough. These forgeries were said to have been quite sophisticated, but, it would appear, not sophisticated enough to halt the interest of King Carlos III in the case.

At this stage, George's wife, daughter and remaining crew were at serious risk back on his ship, which was still moored at his new Port Hillsborough base in the Delta du Saloum. The Jalof tribesmen had watched the ship very closely at anchor offshore and would have seen Glass's departure. With the reduced number of defenders remaining on board, they realised that they now had a great opportunity to capture his ship and whatever might be of value on board. This would have been an enormous prize at a time when their level of poverty was very high. They waited patiently for the right moment and eventually launched no less than three separate attacks on the ship. During fierce fighting to defend themselves, the crew put up a brave defence but in fending off their attackers, some of the Jalof managed to climb on board. Following a great deal of bloodshed on deck, the attackers succeeded in killing the chief officer and six other crew members. It was a blood bath. The terrified Glasses remained hidden below; it is a miracle that Isobell and her daughter survived. Fortunately, the crew were well armed with their muskets and cutlasses and the attackers were eventually beaten off, but at very great cost.

It was now March 1765, almost four months since George Glass left the Port Hillsborough mooring and his wife and daughter. Unfortunately, following the latest attack, the few remaining crew members believed that they did not have the skills to confidently sail and navigate the vessel away from here by themselves. At that time of the year, the Atlantic weather could also be challenging. Losing their chief officer and the other members of the crew made them even more vulnerable. Even a highly skilled crew greatly reduced in size would have struggled to sail the ship. The other option was to do what they could to prepare for the next attack from shore, defend themselves till the end and hope that their food supplies did not run out in the meantime, all in the hope that Captain Glass would soon show up with extra help. Having now lost half of their crew, most likely their attackers would return with a larger number next time. An escape looked not only the wiser option but the only practical one if they were to have any chance of survival. Given the few alternatives, they finally decided that their best option was to lift anchor in the darkness of night and somehow attempt to navigate the journey north in their ship rather than risk using the remaining longboat for their escape. They did have Captain Glass's charts, the ship's compass and some awareness of the key points along the coastline from their earlier journey.

Could they remember their landmarks from the voyage down there and somehow get to safety? Fear and desperation are serious motivators.

They knew that the journey north that they were about to attempt was one of the most dangerous in this part of the world. They would have certainly remembered at least some of Captain George Glass's earlier instructions but not them all. By far the most critical of these was to avoid taking the natural course of hugging the coast, even if it felt safer to be within sight of dry land.

Rising silently in darkness just before dawn the following day, whispering to each other in a fear-driven joint effort, they cautiously lifted their anchor and unfurled their sails. Luckily, a fresh early-morning breeze immediately filled their canvas. Terrified that they might be pursued, all on board kept their eyes glued to the dense mangroves as they pulled away.

Apart from the dawn chorus of sunbirds, longclaws and river prinias, all was quiet. Cautiously they glided silently towards the awaiting Atlantic and began their journey out through almost 200 islands that dotted the Delta du Saloum. As they emerged safely one hour later into the Atlantic, a very strong south-westerly quickly carried them towards their first mark, the Dakar headland. This was not too difficult for them to identify. Sailing downwind now, hour by hour, their confidence in handling the ship began to grow. Glass's charts were also beginning to make more sense to their unaccustomed eyes. At this time in the 1700s, most of the crew would have been illiterate. However, being well educated, this is where Isobell Glass came to their rescue. Her strength of character surprised all. She also did what she could to inspire confidence and tried her best not to transfer her fears to her young daughter, who had no idea that survival was all the remaining crew could think about now. This is also where working as a terrified team was already paying dividends. Some hours later, Cape Verd, to the west, came within their sights. The strong south-westerly winds also continued to help, and within days both Cape Blanco and Cape Bojador slowly drifted by on their starboard side.

Although few of the crew could read, they did have a basic understanding of the ship's charts, and with Isobell's help, they plotted their course ahead from day to day, at all times searching the horizon for any recognisable landmarks. Once they caught sight of the enormous red sand dunes again on their starboard side, they knew that they were at least heading in the right direction. Fortunately, it was still daylight and they could clearly see the jagged shoreline reefs being pounded by towering white surf and they remembered Captain Glass's warning that this was where so many ships made the mistake of sailing too close to shore in times gone by. Bravely, they steered west and out further in to the deep Atlantic before eventually turning north, a tactic that in previous generations had terrified even experienced crews. The weather continued to be kind and the days now passed more quickly, as with so few hands on deck, there was little time for any of them to rest. Although exhausted, spirits rose as they spotted Villa Bens on their starboard side. At this position on their charts, they had to make a very difficult decision. Should they steer west to the Canaries or just keep going north for Spain and Portugal and home? In the open sea, they felt safe. Of course, they did not know if Captain Glass was dead or alive as he had now been missing for months, and surely he would have communicated with them somehow if he was still alive. Encouraged, however, by Isobell, the decision made was to turn west and head over to the Canaries where at least they could rest and seek help.

Isobell Glass and her daughter had survived repeated terrifying attacks at the Delta du Saloum. She witnessed crew members being slaughtered on deck. She worked with the small band of men to learn how to sail a large and somewhat complicated ship, figured out the charts so they could navigate safely to Tenerife, but still she had no idea if her husband was dead or alive.

Once ashore in Tenerife and having immediately reported all to the local authorities, who were not particularly friendly towards the bedraggled and exhausted English crew, details of Isobell's terrifying adventure emerged. It did not take her long to start a search for any news of her husband. While greatly relieved to discover that he was in fact still alive, Isobell was shocked to learn that he had been imprisoned and kept in irons in a dungeon on a starvation diet of bread and water almost from the moment he had set foot on shore in Tenerife over five months earlier. His imprisonment was now widely known as it had received considerable attention once his arrest became public knowledge. Mariners around the busy harbour area would also have been concerned that they, too, could be arrested on some spurious grounds, as it appeared to them that Captain Glass had committed no crime.

Here is the official report of Captain Glass's wife Isobell's ordeal:

> About the same time, March 1765, the settlers at Port Hillsborough were attacked by the blacks, who killed the chief officer and six men. Dreading a renewal of the attack, the survivors made their escape in the boats to Tenerife, where Mrs. Glas first learned of her husband's

detention. Steps appear to have been taken by the British government to obtain his release (ib. par. 2033, no details given), and in October 1765 he was set at liberty.

Isobell must now have been at her wits' end. What state of health was her husband in? Would he have survived his ordeal? However, just like her husband, she was not a quitter and immediately began to make a series of pleadings to the authorities for help. Her efforts made an impact. Following lengthy discussions between the British government and Canary Island authorities, it was the King of Spain who eventually issued an order for his release. George Glass finally walked free in October 1765. In an emotional reunion at the prison gate, under the clock tower of Santa Cruz prison, the captain was reunited with his wife and daughter. Isobell was shocked by her husband's wasted appearance. He had served ten months' hard labour in chains in close confinement and was almost starved to death. The fact that he had spent time in cells on several occasions over the previous fifteen years had probably prevented him from going insane while imprisoned in Tenerife and this possibly saved his life.

4

Heading Home for Christmas

George was greatly weakened by his harsh treatment in prison in Tenerife, but he had other worries too. His ship had been confiscated in the Canaries following his wife's heroic voyage of escape from Port Hillsborough, a costly loss that could have major consequences. His seven crew members had also abandoned him soon after he was arrested and had not been seen since. The only good thing was the happy reunification with his wife and daughter. This tough and experienced mariner's spirit was almost broken. His traumatised wife and young child also just wanted to get home to Dundee to the safety of their friends and family. George had not seen his siblings for some years and had a lot of catching up to do. He

Santa Cruz de Tenerife Port, Canary Islands, Spain

was, however, still very concerned for the safety of his family. He no longer trusted the authorities in the Canaries and had no intention of remaining in Tenerife any longer than was absolutely necessary. The governor of the Canaries, Don Domingo Bernardi Gomez Rabelo, just wanted to get rid of him and the sooner he saw the back of Captain George Glass and his wife, the better.

Determined as ever to make the most of his situation, as soon as George regained his strength, he began the search for a safe passage back home. At the very least, they could now return to a comfortable life in Dundee, or perhaps London. He might even be able to enjoy the wealth he had accumulated and wisely kept here in La Orotava, on Tenerife. During his earlier planning for retirement, he knew that his cessation agreement still had very significant value.

George's extended family in Dundee would also be looking forward to a reunion after all these years. His ten-year-old daughter, too, would finally be able to spend some time with her aging grandfather. No doubt George would have some explaining to do to his financial backers in London, but knowing his record, he would find ways to turn the lucrative agreement he had secured at Port Hillsborough in Senegal to the benefit of all concerned.

While George was recovering his health and regaining some of his lost weight, Isobell filled him in on the details of the long story of her voyage up the west coast of Africa to the Canaries. He most certainly would have been greatly impressed. Her courage and determination were something which he would have greatly admired. Bringing his ship and crew safely back to Tenerife was extraordinary, even if it had been confiscated by Don Domingo Bernardi Gomez Rabelo.

As Christmas was now just some weeks away, they even had time for some family shopping. George treated his wife to a whole new wardrobe and also bought gifts for his daughter, who would soon celebrate her eleventh birthday. It didn't take him very long to sort out travel arrangements for their voyage back to London. The passage he found for their journey home was on board the 120-ton brig, *Earl of Sandwich*. The owner was a Belfast man. The ship was built just three years earlier, in 1762, in Yarmouth in England. The vessel appears in 1764 as one of the earliest entries in Lloyd's Register, and the details there state that her hull, masts and rigging were all in good order. Brigs were bigger than schooners but still relatively small. They varied in length from 75 ft to 165 ft and the *Earl of Sandwich* was in the midrange of 100 ft in length. A crew of eight was recommended by Lloyd's for safe sailing. The fact that it was an almost new vessel would have given him some confidence that his choice of transport home for Christmas was a good one. Their many nightmare experiences of the past year were coming to an end at last. He certainly did not want to have any further mishaps or dramas on the journey home. Although still a young man, it was time to retire and he could afford it.

Because of their relatively small size, the freelance crews of brigs were usually hired locally and often in taverns, boarding houses or just on the quayside close to the docks where the ships were loaded and unloaded and where crews were hired and fired every day of the week. The whole routine was quite a casual one and most experienced skippers, over time, got to know and recognise the hard workers and the shirkers. That was especially the case in Tenerife. Many crews would also have known each other from earlier voyages, and if one was hired, they would try to get their mates on the same ship for company. The docklands of the Canaries had a less obvious nasty side, as the slave trade was flourishing there at that time. Being fairly close to Africa's west coast, slave ships regularly arrived here to replenish their food and water supplies. On arrival, they were usually fully loaded with their sad human cargo on the way from West Africa across the Atlantic to the Americas. Their crews also tended to be more aggressive individuals, better armed and sometimes better paid than those on general trading ships, as they had to be prepared at all times for possible violence on board. Some sailors would opt not to get involved with slave ships to avoid the risks of disease and worse. Mutinies on board were common and so the slaves were shackled below deck at all times. There were anything up to 600 or 700 slaves packed so tightly side by side that the arrangement was referred to as the spoon position. Driven by profit, it was a miserable life-threatening existence for all involved, both above and below deck. Everyone was exposed to sea sickness, disease and even death.

Captain William Cockeran of the *Earl of Sandwich* had only just sailed from London to Santa Cruz, Tenerife, with a cargo of bale-goods, hardware, hats and other dry goods. Once unloaded, he continued on to nearby Orotava. According to Lloyd's Register, the vessel had previously docked in Cadiz in Andalusia in Spain. As usual, Captain Cockeran hired an assorted group of sailors in Tenerife to serve under him on this next journey back to London. Cockeran, too, had earlier served his time on slave ships and was known to be a capable but tough skipper. Some of the newly hired crew may have already been known to Cockeran as he was a regular visitor to

Tenerife. Whether Captain George Glass and he had crossed paths prior to this, we do not know.

Records show that the crew of the *Earl of Sandwich* comprised English mariners George Gidley and the less experienced twenty-year-old Yorkshire-born Richard St Quinten, described as "a man of slow apprehension", Irishman Peter MacKinlie, and Andrew Zekerman, referred to as the tall Dutchman, although he may have been German. Other deckhands hired by Captain Cockeran for the journey were the mate Charles Pinchent and his young brother James. Captain Cockeran also took on twelve-year-old Benjamin Gallispey as his own personal cabin boy. George Glass, too, brought a young cabin boy to help his wife and child. In addition to the three members of the Glass family and Captain Cockeran, there was now a total crew of six plus the young cabin boys, more or less the number recommended for safety by Lloyd's Register for a 120-ton vessel.

In searching for and selecting his crew for the voyage, it would have been routine for Captain Cockeran to ensure that their roles were clearly defined from the start and matched their skills and experience. Most important of all was the position of bosun. He would report directly to Captain Cockeran and be responsible for all the crew and equipment on board. This critical position was filled by the Irishman Peter MacKinlie. Although not a tall man, he had a fearsome reputation and tended to command through intimidation. He carried a sword at all times. Although Captain Cockeran may have known him from previous visits to Tenerife and may even have hired him in the past, he might not have been fully aware that this man was an unpredictable individual and a heavy drinker, a sometimes dangerous combination of traits in any situation and especially at sea. Englishman George Gidley was hired as the cook and overseer of all the provisions on board, a major responsibility at sea as any theft of food supplies was always severely punished. Captain Cockeran was known to be a very experienced disciplinarian and while this would have appealed to George Glass, it should have made the bosun and cook wary and to avoid trouble. Cockeran had been at sea since he was a young boy and was well able to tell the difference between those who could manage the task ahead and any thieves and beggars looking for easy employment on the docks as they wandered from ship to ship looking for work.

Passenger George Glass would have quickly sized up the abilities of both the crew and skipper and would be better at spotting potential trouble than most. The combined talents of Captain Cockeran and the bosun, Peter MacKinlie, would have given no reason for concern on this voyage. Unlike many who would have travelled through Tenerife, Captain Cockeran also had a solid reputation as an honest and trustworthy man in both London and Tenerife, despite the fact that his career included time spent as an officer on slave ships. As was the experience of George Glass during his time at sea, investors back in London highly valued men of integrity like Captain William Cockeran. Funding trade, as we know, was an expensive and risky business when both pirates and opposing navies frequently took advantage of small ships such as the *Earl of Sandwich*. Certainly, the Belfast owner of this ship wanted his asset to be in safe hands. The brig appeared to have little of real value on board at this time, other than its paying passengers. The manifest included barrels of sweet Malmsey Madeira wine, raw and manufactured silk and cochineal, a much sought after scarlet dye. The unusual pipe barrels had a tapered top and bottom and each could hold about one hundred gallons. These were heavy and needed to be tightly roped together below deck to prevent the ship from listing in bad weather. Even William Shakespeare is known to have had a special fondness for Malmsey wine from the Canaries!

Brigs such as the *Earl of Sandwich* were recognised as fast and manoeuvrable and ideal for the relatively short journey ahead. Because of that, they were also used for both naval and trading purposes at that time and were easy to handle for experienced crews. Some brigs were even used for whaling and sealing, they were so versatile. Because of this, in the great navies of the eighteenth and nineteenth century, they served as couriers for battle fleets and as training vessels for cadets. A voyage with little cargo of value and just a few paying passengers on board was very much an insignificant task for this vessel.

In preparing for the voyage to London, the crew of the *Earl of Sandwich* would have worked hard for a few days before departure loading and securing the general cargo against the typical November sea conditions in the Bay of Biscay and beyond as they headed north. Personal items were often loaded separately by other dockers as these would usually be stored in whatever private accommodation was provided on board rather than down in the cargo hold. Under clear blue skies, only the kestrels circling above showed any interest in their work, at the same time hoping to swoop on the occasional lizard warming its body on the rocky Canaries shoreline. The crew would also have adjusted the ballast material as required below deck to ensure that the ship was stable, well balanced and not listing before they left the harbour. The large ballast ports just above the water line made it easier for the crew to load or unload the ballast material, often just rocks that were readily available nearby; in this case they were volcanic rocks. As was the custom, the captain told his crew to enjoy their final night on shore. Mariners were at their most dangerous at these times ashore and often feared by the local communities in the port areas. Drunkenness and violence were part of their lifestyle ashore. And so as the sun set and the ship was now fully prepared for sailing the following morning, Captain Cockeran was quite happy to stay away from the local taverns and to be left alone on board. He had urgent business that did not need prying eyes. His reputation for honesty is confirmed by the unknown and unlisted cargo that had earlier been carried on board and safely concealed in his private quarters. The owners trusted him to both transport and hide the contents and to bring all safely back to London on this last voyage of the year before Christmas.

It is just as well that Cockeran decided not to join his crew ashore. He would have been shocked if he was within earshot of his bosun, MacKinlie, at that moment. MacKinlie was buying large quantities of drinks for all the crew in a local tavern, which was totally out of character for him, but he had a purpose. At some stage, when Gidley, St Quinten and Zekerman were "well oiled", he boasted that he had heard that there was something very special on board the *Earl of Sandwich.* He may well have known some of the dockers who were hired earlier to load personal items for storage in the private compartments of the ship and had picked up some gossip. In their semi-drunken state, MacKinlie gathered them all together saying that they should all join him in taking control the ship during the coming days and steal for themselves what he thought was a valuable cargo on board. He boasted that as they sailed for London, this was their opportunity to prepare for a well-deserved retirement after all their years of hardship, rough treatment and low pay at sea. How he had come across this information, even if it was true, we do not know. It may have been just drunken bluster, or perhaps another mariner had passed the word to him on the dockside. Either way, this was very dangerous talk. This conversation alone was enough to have them all put in chains or worse. Such talk on drunken nights before sailing were often just sheer bravado and not taken too seriously. Fortunately for them, MacKinlie and the crew were not overheard by others, and as alcohol took over, the banter drifted to their other experiences at sea, the barmaids and what they would all do for Christmas when they reached London.

The captain and his crew slept well on board later that night. First up on the morning of their departure was Cockeran. He quickly unpacked his seldom used frock coat and sword, of which he was very proud, as he wanted to look his best for their departure. Then he went above deck to take command of the *Earl of Sandwich*. He was most likely also aware that his passenger Captain George Glass would arrive early looking his best too in his formal naval jacket and sword. The smell of alcohol fumes below deck that morning would have caused an explosion if a match was struck. MacKinlie began by reminding everyone that he was the most senior officer below Captain Cockeran, and before long he was barking out orders left, right and centre, turning the ship in to a hive of activity both above and below deck. Checking the running rigging, shrouds, stays, sheets, spars, halyards, braces, ropes, chains, ship's ballast and all the vital sailing equipment was his responsibility.

As always, the moment of departure was an exciting one. George Glass arrived with his family on the dockside for last-minute boarding. It must have been an impressive sight. George, wearing his smart naval uniform and ceremonial sword, his elegant, attractive wife and their young daughter, all made their way up the gangway to be welcomed by the equally elegant Captain William Cockeran. While much of their luggage had already been loaded the evening before, Isobell and her daughter had done some last-minute shopping, which the crew now kindly carried up the gangway.

The relatively new vessel must have looked impressive, with her three-mast design and enormous, square, heavy furled canvas rigging, as she rested at anchor under blue skies in the warm November air. The accommodation towards the stern provided for Captain Glass and his family would have been small but reasonably comfortable, and that was also the quieter part of the vessel. As this journey was not a very long one compared with their recent travels, they would have put up without complaint with such things as uncomfortable bunks and cramped quarters for the duration. All were certainly looking forward to a Christmas together at home.

Although the voyage was, on the face of it, very much a routine one, unknown to anyone except Captain Cockeran, the cargo really was extraordinary. A concealed armoured chest weighing almost two tons was now well hidden in the Captains private quarters. He had hired the help of others to carry this on board before his own crew began the loading of the general cargo. Confirmed by *The Journal of the Royal Historical and Archaeological Association of Ireland* (Fourth

Series, Vol. 8), in today's money, the contents would have an estimated value of over £20,000,000. The reason why this chest was so heavy and needed to be secreted on board and not in view of the crew was that gold is heavier than lead. This was a real treasure trove and security was absolutely vital. The weight of the armoured chest might have alerted his crew and this was not something Cockeran could or would disclose to anybody. He was confident that he had managed to get this chest on board and successfully concealed without his crew's knowledge.

This enormous fortune on board was now in his trust which said a great deal for his reputation as a skipper. If he thought for one moment that any of the crew were aware of such a quantity of Spanish silver milled dollars, gold ingots, gold dust, precious stones and exotic jewellery, he would not have sailed with them on board. It is unlikely that even George Glass and his family were aware of this enormously heavy oak chest and its contents, as having it on board did increase the element of danger for all of them. Pirates hiding not too far away at the island of La Graciosa would have risked all to get their hands on this treasure.

Also unknown to many, George Glass brought with him a quantity of his own substantial wealth. And so, all in all, this was indeed a very valuable cargo on its way to London and not just a routine voyage. Our guess is that Glass would have asked Captain Cockeran to store his valuables safely for the duration rather than leave them in his family quarters. We must still wonder why the vessel did not even have dedicated armed guards on board. In fact it should really have had a fully armed escort ship for security. The authorities probably hoped that a well-concealed cargo would go unnoticed and would slip through the shipping lanes and not be the subject of gossip and arouse the attention of prowling pirates and privateers. In the 1700s, fortunes could not simply be transferred from bank to bank or from government to government as paper transactions. The precious transactions relied on transport to get from point to point and in this case, it was on board the *Earl of Sandwich.*

But one member of the crew had already guessed that there was something of great value on the vessel.

PART TWO
THE MAYHEM

O Peter, sure you will not serve me this.

CAPTAIN GEORGE GLASS

5

Mutiny on Board

Bosun MacKinlie was known to be the most feared crew member on board the *Earl of Sandwich*. None of the others had the courage to warn the skipper about his declared intention to take control of the ship and steal its cargo. Perhaps, they didn't take his drunken talk seriously and just forgot about it overnight.

Casting off in late November 1765 and pulling out of the port of La Orotava on the northern side of Tenerife, the three year-old vessel would have looked impressive as it finally departed. One person in particular was no doubt delighted to see George Glass leave: Governor Don Domingo Bernardi

Port Town of Orotava, Santa Cruz de Tenerife, Canary Islands, Spain

Gomez Rabelo, the person responsible for his arrest and detention earlier and which almost cost him his life. Losing face with the King of Spain was not something the governor would ever forgive or easily forget. Don Domingo Bernardi Gomez Rabelo may even have travelled to La Orotava that morning just to make sure that this troublesome Scotsman had at last departed.

The ship headed north, and sailing conditions were good as they rounded the coast of Tenerife and passed Fuerteventura and Lanzarote, before setting a course north-east towards North Africa. Any pirates lurking in the usual hiding places around the island of La Graciosa would not have seen this target as worth the effort. Any spies they had in port had nothing of interest to report, it appeared.

George Glass and his wife, now well used to these sailing routines, had quickly unpacked and settled well in their quarters. Their young daughter, by this time, was also well used to the rolling motion of the *Earl of Sandwich* and played with some new toys her parents had bought for her the day before.

Once they had cleared the north coast of Tenerife, all they would have seen was the vast expanse of the open sea ahead. The daily routine was quickly established. Captain Cockeran and MacKinlie appeared to work well together. Following an uneventful first day at sea, and before nightfall, they already had the far-away lights of Casablanca and Morocco on their starboard side. Their next major landmark would be the Strait of Gibraltar, where the two continents are separated by just nine miles. From that location, they would head further north and up the coast of Portugal. This general area was still heavily patrolled by armed naval ships from Spain, France and

Britain, and pirates would have kept their distance. Captain
Cockeran more than likely felt a level of security from this
incidental protection.

Early the next day, while Captain Cockeran was at the
helm and the Glass family was still resting in their quarters
below deck, as soon as bosun MacKinlie made sure that the
crew had finished their early-morning chores, the small group
of Gidley, Zekerman and St Quinten gathered around him for
a whispered conversation. MacKinlie brought the subject back
to their drunken banter during their final night in port to see
how many would now, in broad daylight, support his scheme
to locate whatever valuable treasure there might be on board.
Surprisingly, all but the young Richard St Quinten were more
than eager to hear how this plan might work, even if they
still didn't take it seriously. After answering a few questions,
MacKinlie broke away as he was aware that Captain Cockeran
could now see them and might be suspicious.

Making good progress, the brig's course now took them
slowly north towards Lisbon on that long run up the length of
Portugal's coast. Hugging the coastline, as most skippers did
in those days, they next passed the bright city lights of Porto,
where the Douro River enters the Atlantic. The *Earl of Sandwich*
was now getting close to entering the Bay of Biscay. At some
point here, the tall and intimidating Andres Zekerman pulled
the younger reluctant crew member, Richard St Quinten,
aside. He made it very clear to the young man that he, Peter
MacKinlie and George Gidley, wanted St Quinten to join them
in taking over the ship and its possible rich cargo in due course.
He sensed that St Quinten was nervous but again made it clear
that they could all live in luxury for the rest of their lives, and
this opportunity might never present itself again. St Quinten is

known to have had a hard life at sea as a young freelance sailor. Mariners tended not to survive till old age which was regarded then as surviving past your fortieth birthday. His upbringing had presented him with the possibility of several careers but he never seemed to finish the apprenticeships undertaken or gain the necessary experience he needed to achieve a steady income. Born in Yorkshire in the north of England, he was just nineteen years of age at the time of this fateful voyage. He had previously worked for a Dublin ship owner and gained the reputation of being reliable. That led him eventually to being hired by Captain Cockeran for this passage. MacKinlie, too, was eager that the young man agree, as the plan he had in mind required a team of four to have any chance of success. According to a statement St Quinten made later, he did not fully believe what MacKinlie or Zekerman were proposing at this stage. Before Zekerman finished what was regarded by St Quinten as an intimidating conversation, he warned him that he was to keep his mouth shut. Later the young man must have reconsidered the hard life on board these ships, the poor pay and the constant threat of punishment. The prospect of an alternative to this lifestyle must have at least been worth considering. This might be one opportunity he could see through to the end. In all of these conversations, the young brothers Charles and James Pinchent and the two cabin boys were excluded and were totally unaware of the scheming in progress.

At breakfast the next morning, when the crew gathered as usual below deck, St Quinten was warned by the others yet again that if he mentioned the plan to anybody, he would die. The young lad was terrified at this stage. As the junior deckhand, he was also well aware of the punishments of the time for mutiny. This was an enormous decision for any of these men to take. They were putting their lives at serious risk.

It became evident that soon after their departure from Tenerife, both George Gidley, the cook, and Peter MacKinlie, the bosun, had stolen a quantity of the ship's Canary Island wine, an expensive luxury at that time. This had already put both of them at serious risk of punishment. As exposure for this crime and the resultant consequences were now imminent, they probably felt they had nothing to lose. Even the stealing of food could warrant a death sentence. It is surprising that Captain Cockeran had not spotted this transgression already as they had to work very closely together on deck and both the affect and the smell of alcohol in such confined spaces are difficult to hide.

That evening, the mutiny plan was finally ready to go. The night was chilly, the sky was cloudy and darkness came early. Timing was critical. The growing tension on board among the men went unnoticed by the captain and his passengers. The mutineers somehow needed to get Captain Cockeran on deck by himself to begin their attack, but that didn't happen and they were forced to postpone the plan for now. The decision was to wait till later and select a location nearer to a coastline where they could somehow get rid of their passengers.

The following morning, the tension eased just a little. But with some time to relax on deck on this routine passage in fair weather conditions, the mutiny was secretly discussed again later in the afternoon. This time, the plan was agreed with more enthusiasm by all, including St Quinten. The *Earl of Sandwich* was now making slow progress through the rough seas of the Bay of Biscay and at times appeared to be making no progress at all. Such conditions often make crews even more stressed. With cargoes breaking lose below deck, the task of constantly securing them on the brig as it rolled and pitched was a dangerous one, and injuries often occurred. On this voyage, so far they were coping well.

It is worth considering the harsh and somewhat cruel environment in which these men lived in the late 1700s. Their short life expectancy and general hardships were a major part of their day. The decisions the crew made were driven by the desperation created by the constant suffering that was part of their way of life. The penalties for theft on board that hung over them were severe. The actual punishment methods were well established by England's Royal Navy and carried out without mercy. These set the standard which many skippers followed. Almost any crime committed on board could earn a flogging. The standard whip used had nine knotted strings of leather known as the cat-o'-nine-tails. Cabin boys as young as eleven or twelve were flogged with a shorter five-tail whip. The guilty party was first put in leg irons on the upper deck, where he was given the long, narrow strips of leather and forced to make the cat-o'-nine-tails to be used to inflict punishment on his own back later. If he refused, his punishment was simply increased. Twenty-four hours later and still in leg irons, the punishment process began in earnest. The entire crew was first assembled and details of the crime read aloud as a deterrent to others. The perpetrator was tied bare-chested to part of the rigging, and, standing an arm's length away, the bosun or his mate usually carried out the whipping. Using the strength of a full swing, twelve lashes were administered. If more than one crime was involved, a further set of twelve lashes was delivered for each crime. Often the administers were rotated, alternating between a right-handed and a left-handed crew member. This produced a criss-crossed and more painful flesh wound. Following this, the sailor was dragged below deck where seawater, salt or vinegar was rubbed in to the lacerated skin. This was often even more painful than the flogging, and sometimes the shock even caused death. The stated justification for the use of salt or vinegar was that it prevented infection. England's Royal Navy continued to use this punishment till as late as 1881.

Mutiny, considered to be one of the most serious crimes of all at sea, was a hanging offence, but not as we might know it. Crew members were again assembled on deck to hear details of the crime read aloud and to witness the punishment. A noose was placed around the neck of the accused, whose hands and feet were first bound. The victim was then slowly hauled up on the yardarm, a spar on the mast of the square-rigged sails high above, by members of the crew. Death from this gradual strangulation was very slow and very painful. The body was not returned to the deck till one hour later.

Another punishment for mutiny for the four men to consider was keel-hauling. In that case, a rope was passed below the hull of the vessel from one side to the other. The victim's hands and feet were bound and he was then tied to one end of the rope and tossed over the side. The crew then pulled him under the keel and up the other side as quickly as they could but not as quickly as the unfortunate victim would have liked. While being dragged under the keel, which would have been covered in barnacles and other shells acting like razors, we can only imagine the pain to be endured, even if he could hold his breath for the time needed to survive the haul. This is an academic point as many sailors could not swim anyway.

Andres Zekerman, Peter MacKinlie, George Gidley and the doubtful Richard St Quinten really did have a great deal to consider. Failure of their plan was destined to have dire consequences for each and every one of them. The reason piracy and mutiny were punished so harshly at this time was that some of those pirates and privateers were very well organised and posed a serious threat to global trade and to those who financed that trade as we learned from the earlier mayhem caused by the pirate Henry Every. Another example was the infamous Mr Edward Teach, also known as Blackbeard the Pirate, who had no less than four well-armed ships under his command and a private army of over 300 men. His own 200-ton ship had sixteen cannons. He even succeeded in defeating several ships of the British Navy. In spite of all efforts to rid the seas of pirates it still continued and the authorities were determined to stamp it out, hence the very severe punishments. Like George Glass, Blackbeard also began his career at sea as a privateer.

Nine days after their departure from the Port of Orotava, they had completed most of their two-week journey. To break their voyage following a very rough crossing of the Bay of Biscay, as they headed north and left the coast of France, Captain Cockeran, on Thursday, 21 November 1765, decided to head for the small fishing village of Crookhaven in West Cork, on Ireland's south coast, for a brief rest and to top up their provisions. Locals on shore may have been alarmed by this approaching vessel, and with good reason, even if the incident took place in the previous century. On 20 June 1631, two ships under the command of the infamous pirate Murat Reis dropped anchor in the middle of the night near the coastal town of Baltimore in West Cork. Early the following

morning, over 200 armed pirates caught the town completely
by surprise, torched their thatched cottages, rounded up over
100 men, women and children, both Irish villagers and new
English settlers, and carried them off to the slave markets of
North Africa, never to be heard of again. A similar raid took
place in Cornwall some years later. In the 1600s, Crookhaven
was an early English Plantation fishing colony that also became
a notorious haven for pirates, hence its name. To counteract
this activity, lighthouses, watchtowers and excise men were
later placed there in an attempt to restore some semblance
of law and order to the area. However, in 1765, it was still a
somewhat notorious place with very little for resting crews to
do to pass the time other than head for the many ale houses
and create some mayhem.

During the six-day stay of the crew of the *Earl of Sandwich* in
Crookhaven, to discourage the smuggling of tea and tobacco
and other commodities along this jagged coastline, a customs
officer came on board the ship to check for contraband as
was quite normal at that time. This would involve a thorough
search both above and below deck, and these customs officers,
often retired mariners, knew where contraband was most
likely to be concealed. There is no record of what happened
when the officer inspected Captain Cockeran's private
quarters or how he might have responded to finding out what
the enormous armoured chest actually contained which was
concealed beneath a heavy velvet cloth.

True to form, although it was still early morning, MacKinlie
was already drunk on more stolen wine. Did Captain Cockeran
turn a blind eye to this behaviour? Stupidly, the drunken
bosun even boasted to the customs officer, giving some details
of the plan to take over the ship. Knowing the recent history

and reputation of Crookhaven and being greatly alarmed and also well aware of the seriousness of such a crime, the customs officer immediately reported what he had heard to Captain Cockeran. For some extraordinary reason, which we will never understand, the Captain did not believe the officer. Since the Captain was armed and as it was a relatively small ship and he had personally faced down troublesome crews before and survived, he possibly thought that if there was a threat, he could handle it. He would also have had the full support of the imposing figure of passenger Captain George Glass, who carried his own sword at all times. The remaining three-day journey to England was also a short one, and the atmosphere on board had been reasonably good since their departure from Tenerife, or so Captain Cockeran thought.

It was time now for the final leg of their journey. George Glass and his family would soon be celebrating Christmas at home with their relatives, whom they had not seen for several years. Their daughter was approaching her birthday and would no doubt be spoiled by her grandparents, uncles and aunts. She still had to finish that delicate embroidery on her sampler that was to be given as a present to one lucky relative.

On Tuesday, 26 November 1765, the *Earl of Sandwich* finally lifted anchor and departed Crookhaven for the last leg of their journey. Typical winds at that time of the year would have been light south-westerlies, with a temperature of around 50°F. In other words, these were good, firm sailing conditions.

Friday, 29 November 1765, was a very happy day for the Glass family. The Captain's wife Isobell and her daughter, rose early. With the end of their voyage in sight, they were going to enjoy a special celebration. The happy Glass family event included young Benjamin Gallispey and the Glass cabin boy, both close to young Catherine's age, as it was time to enjoy the young girl's eleventh birthday. This was an important moment for the Glass parents as they had all rarely been together for such occasions. Wearing some of the new clothes which her father had bought for her before their departure, they all sang 'happy birthday' and the presents were opened. George's wife also kindly had some small gifts for the overjoyed youngsters, Benjamin Gallispey and the Glass cabin boy. When the little event was over and the presents tidied away, much to the joy of her parents, young Catherine continued her needlework on her sampler as she really wanted to finish it before reaching London.

The following night, Saturday, 30 November, the air was chilly and all was quiet below deck. The brig was now travelling approximately seventy nautical miles per day as they approached the English Channel. Captain Glass, his wife and their daughter had retired early to get some rest before, hopefully, disembarking the next day. At 10.00 p.m. and in pitch darkness, while making good progress on this relatively calm but cold night, the ship was now just thirty miles south-west of Old Grimsby in the Isles of Scilly. Penzance, Falmouth and Plymouth lay straight ahead. They were nearly home.

As the Glass family slept peacefully in their quarters at the stern, below deck MacKinlie and the others were in a state of high anxiety. In their scheming minds, they had now arrived at the point of no return as time had just about run out. Their plan, which already had several false starts, now had to be abandoned or carried out. If they did not take action tonight, it would be too late. They knew only too well that their theft of wine during the voyage meant that serious punishment for them was already certain, and this would all come to a head anyway as soon as they reached Gravesend on the south bank of the Thames Estuary, when the missing wine would be discovered. Jumping ship might be a possibility but thieves were often rounded up later and getting work on other ships with a record of theft was never going to be easy.

It all began when the constantly inebriated MacKinlie casually ambled over to the quarter deck area in the darkness of that November night. On the pretence of checking the compass, MacKinlie slowly approached Captain Cockeran, who was enjoying these last hours of the voyage while on duty at the wheel. As soon as the moment was right, MacKinlie suddenly grabbed the captain around the middle from behind as strongly as he could and with all his strength lifted him into the air. Taken totally by surprise, the captain immediately put up a fierce struggle to free himself. Both were strong men. Both knew this was serious. While MacKinlie was not a tall man, much shorter than Captain Cockeran, his years of labouring at sea had made him stronger than most. Very quickly, as the Captain swung around and loosened MacKinlie's grip, it looked like he was going to overpower the bosun who had now spent his initial advantage of surprise. That would have spelled the end of their treacherous plan. It would also have meant certain death by hanging for MacKinlie for assaulting his captain. Fists punching and legs kicking, they fell together and rolled across the deck, banging in to a hatch cover, screaming and gouging, each trying desperately to overcome the other. Watching close by, as planned, George Gidley, the ship's cook, panicked. He too could see that it was not supposed to happen like this. They were all about to be exposed if the captain overpowered MacKinlie, and Cockeran was now getting the upper hand. Terror had taken over. Holding as tightly as he could to a long, heavy and cold iron bar which he had earlier concealed on deck, just in case it might be needed, Gidley ran towards the desperate scuffle. As the combatants continued to fight and desperately punch each other, Gidley waited for the right moment. Raising the heavy bar high in the air, and with all the force which he could muster, he landed it squarely on the head of the unfortunate captain. The force of the blow was so great that the captain's skull instantly shattered. In a pool of blood and bone and grey brain matter, he lay dead without time for even a final prayer. Partly in shock, MacKinlie now released his grip on Captain Cockeran and, for a few moments, just lay beside the corpse, stunned and breathless. The ship's skipper was a lifeless and shocking sight. The iron bar which was still in the hands of George Gidley had done more damage than even he thought possible. MacKinlie, too, was covered in the captain's splattered blood as he scrambled unsteadily to his feet. The stark reality of what they had just done caused them both to stare in disbelief at the carnage on deck before the next phase of their mutiny re-entered their thoughts.

By this time, the "man of slow apprehension", Richard St Quinten, had been awakened by the commotion as he slept in the forecastle crew quarters in the bow of the ship and had not realised that the mutiny plan was already in progress. He quickly ran towards the stern, guessing what had commenced from the enormous commotion on deck, where he joined MacKinlie and Gidley and saw the carnage. He was immediately commanded to help. The three of them, working together, then proceeded to lift the heavy corpse of Captain William Cockeran, carry him over to the gunwale and dump him overboard. In a soft and almost silent splash, he was gone.

The mayhem continued.

There had been far too much commotion on deck for all the others on board not to know by now that something dreadful was happening. Had they collided with another vessel? Hit some floating jetsam? Sprung a leak? Or even run aground? Not knowing what to expect, the young brothers Charles and James Pinchent scrambled out of their bunks and made their way quickly to the scene. We can only imagine their shock when the young lads first saw the pools of blood on the wet deck. Gidley still had the blood-covered iron bar in his hands. Without warning, Gidley then swung the bar at the head of Charles Pinchent, who quickly ducked to escape a deadly blow as his brother ran to escape the bloodshed. In the continuing panic, as Gidley again swiped the bar at the head of young Charles, it flew out of his bloodied hands, bounced three times across the deck, toppled over the gunwales and fell into the sea below. Gidley screamed for St Quinten to help, and together they grabbed and pummelled Charles Pinchent and pinned him to the deck. Once he was subdued and dazed, Gidley and St Quinten lifted up the poor lad and also flung him overboard. James Pinchent had by now disappeared from sight in his attempt to save his own life.

Not surprisingly, George Glass and his family were also wide awake in their cabin some distance away at the stern of the vessel. Glass immediately knew that the commotion above was serious. He jumped out of bed, dressed as quickly as he could while warning his wife to lock their cabin door securely behind him and not to open it till he returned. Instead of charging up on deck using the main stairway, Glass was more cautious and quietly climbed the ladder nearest to the family's cabin door. Peaking carefully above deck, while doing his best to stay out of sight, it did not take him long to recognise what was going on. Even though the night was dark, the large amount of blood glistening on the oak deck planking was enough to tell the whole story. He had survived mutinies before.

His instinct told him to immediately return to his cabin and grab his sword. But MacKinlie had already guessed that at some stage Glass would arrive on deck and would pose a very serious challenge to their mutiny. In fact, MacKinlie had spotted him just before he ran to his cabin for his sword. Anticipating that Glass would quickly return from his quarters with his weapon, MacKinlie calmly hid in the shadows beneath the ladder leading up to the deck above. After telling his terrified wife once again to keep their cabin door firmly locked, the now well-armed Glass rushed back to the ladder. When he was just halfway up, MacKinlie sprang out from his hiding place, grabbed Glass by his left arm with all his strength, and once off balance, swung him around. In one fierce swipe, he "ript open his body with a knife". The wound was so deep that Glass's vital organs spilled out.

It was revealed in testimony later that at that moment Captain George Glass exclaimed aloud, "O Peter, sure you will not serve me this." As Glass's blood gushed from the fatal stomach wound, MacKinlie screamed for help. St Quinten was first to arrive. He grabbed the sword still held loosely in the dying man's hand, and with no hesitation or consideration whatsoever, lunged it cruelly into George Glass's body not once but three times. Such hatred from St Quinten was extraordinary. Sharing time during this voyage, watching George Glass and his family on deck, perhaps even joining in the singing of 'happy birthday' to young Catherine the day before, now all turned to a cold blooded and cowardly murder!

Those final dying words of Captain George Glass to his murderer, Peter MacKinlie, tell us a great deal about both his nature and humanity : "O Peter, sure you will not serve me this."

What a tragic and demeaning end for such an unusual man of enormous talent and achievement, a man who had survived so many extreme challenges both on land and at sea over his forty years on earth. He did not even have time to say goodbye to his wife or young daughter, who lay just a few paces away behind the locked door of their cabin. This ship's surgeon, naval officer, adventurer, entrepreneur, privateer, author, explorer, family man and husband, died cruelly and without mercy at the hands of heartless mutineers on what should have been an enjoyable and safe passage home for Christmas. To add even further to this dreadful family tragedy, Captain Glass had earlier found time to send a letter to his father, Reverend John Glas, who was in Perth in Scotland at that time, and informed him that they were all heading home. As with any family, everyone would have been counting the days to the greatly anticipated moment of joyful reunion.

But the savagery on board the *Earl of Sandwich* did not end there.

Gidley next wrenched George Glass's bloodied sword from St Quinten, who was still gazing in shock at the slain man as he laid lifeless beside the ladder leading to the upper deck. Armed with the weapon, Gidley set off to find James Pinchent, the mate's brother who escaped to hide when Charles was thrown overboard moments earlier. Try as he might, Gidley could not find him. In exasperation, Gidley screamed for MacKinlie's help. Apart from being the main conspirator, MacKinlie appeared to have been involved in almost every element of the bloody mayhem and cruelty of the night. Eventually, the pair managed to corner the terrified young James on deck, and during the fierce struggle which followed, MacKinlie suffered a serious injury to his arm. Nevertheless, he and Gidley were too strong for the young lad and finally overpowered him. They then dragged James kicking and screaming across the deck and hurled him over the gunwales and into the cold, dark sea below to join his brother in his watery grave.

The body count was mounting. It now included the ship's skipper, William Cockeran, Captain George Glass, Charles Pinchent and his brother James Pinchent.

Up to this point, Isobell and her daughter were too terrified to venture out of their cabin. Her husband had warned her to stay there till he returned. While they would have heard the shouts, screams and banging on the main deck above, and all the commotion outside their cabin door, they could never have imagined what savagery had really taken place. They awaited the return of Glass to their cabin to confirm that all was now safe. Isobell is very unlikely to have heard the nearby dying words of her husband, even though the ladder to the upper deck was close to the cabin where she and her daughter were still secured.

Once all was silent again, not knowing what to expect, as Isobell Glass was a capable woman who had handled very well a great deal of adversity at sea over the past year, she could not wait any longer to see what was happening above on deck. Cautiously, she unlocked their cabin door and emerged into the dark and narrow corridor. Holding her daughter firmly behind her for safety, it took her just a few moments to comprehend what lay in front of her. Isobell must have gasped as she spotted the enormous pool of blood now running from the bottom of the ladder towards their quarters. Seconds later, she first recognised the buckled shoes and then his spread-eagled legs facing her and finally came upon the shocking sight of her husband and partner, his torso ripped open, his distinctive blue jacket torn and three massive sword wounds in his chest, his eyes staring and his face as white as a sheet. What a terrifying sight for both wife and daughter to witness.

In her state of total shock, she climbed carefully to the upper deck, tightly squeezing the hand of her little girl, to find out what had happened. As she approached the crew, they gathered sheepishly in a cowardly huddle. Her commanding presence caught them by surprise. After some hesitation, they attempted to explain that her husband had been out of his mind and tried to kill everyone on board and that they just had to retaliate. Isobell was in total disbelief. This was not the behaviour of the man she knew so well and admired so much. Her piercing screams caused them to back off and could be heard from bow to stern and heightened the pure sense of terror on board. All kept their eyes on the grieving mother and terrified daughter, some showing signs of shame. Standing there watching the pitiful pair, the crew knew only too well that the killing of women on board brought bad luck to any vessel. This superstition was deeply ingrained in their souls. But not even that deterred the godless MacKinlie. Having by now taken over the wheel on the poop deck above, immediately on hearing the terrified woman's piercing screams and the pitiful crying of her eleven year-old daughter, MacKinlie roared down to Zekerman, "Throw her overboard. You've not done anything yet!" Without batting an eyelid, the tall strong Dutchman, in one swift movement, roughly lifted off their feet the delicate frames of both Isobell and her young daughter. Carrying them together as they struggled and cried for mercy while clinging desperately to each other, on reaching the gunwales, Zekerman, as if disposing of some unwanted baggage, cast both mother and child overboard, watching casually as they clung to each other and quickly disappeared in to the cold November sea below. It must have been a truly horrible death as they clung together in vain and sank below without a trace on that dreadful, dreadful night. Even the other murderers had to look away as the two helpless lives were taken without mercy. This location just south-west of the Isles of Scilly had certainly never before witnessed such a sight of heartless carnage.

Wasting no time, the mutineers next went below and dragged the heavy dead body of Captain George Glass up the main ladder and onto the deck. Totally without compassion, they quickly set about stripping his body of his embroidered blue frock coat, pocket watch, shoes, buckles and anything else of value. Gidley casually wiped some blood from the captain's distinctive and ripped jacket, and although it was far too big for his smaller frame, he put it on as if it was his very own. Once they had relieved the corpse of all personal items, it took the four of them to lift the tall man and unceremoniously throw him overboard to join all the other innocent victims of the past hour or so at the bottom of the sea. At this point, apart from the four mutineers, only the cabin boy, twelve-year-old Benjamin Gallispey, and the Glass family's young servant boy remained alive. By this time, St Quinten had taken over the wheel from MacKinlie who commanded him to turn the vessel around and to steer a course north-west as they trimmed the sails to remove themselves from this busy shipping area as quickly as possible. Having murdered Captain Cockeran, their problem now was that they had also lost his navigation skills. Neither could they call on Captain George Glass to provide advice. They would just have to hope for the best and see where the winds might take them. Most of all, they needed to act quickly to avoid capture or worse.

6

Pirates Risk all for Treasure

The 120-ton *Earl of Sandwich* now headed back in the direction of Ireland's south-east coast, following a relatively short passage across the Irish Sea. On the horizon the mutineers could already see a faint impression of the approaching coastline. Overcoming their lack of navigation skills was probably more a matter of luck than design. As they had no wish to face the authorities on English soil in the area of the Bristol Channel to their stern, and being fully aware of the severe penalties facing them, they now dropped anchor to gather their thoughts. It was approximately seventeen miles to the shores ahead. Even though bosun MacKinlie was Irish, his knowledge of local geography appears to have been very limited, and they were still not sure of their exact position in the Irish Sea.

MacKinlie had suffered a severe arm injury during the struggle to capture young James Pinchent, and he was bleeding heavily. He now held his position at the wheel and commanded the other mutineers to go below and wash the blood stains from their clothes, shoes and hands. They would also try as best they could to take care of their own injuries. Once St Quinten returned, MacKinlie posted him at the wheel and proceeded to lead the others straight to the skipper's quarters, believing that this was where a precious cargo of some sort must be hidden. They were certainly not disappointed. Beside the captain's chart table, beneath a heavy velvet cover, sat an enormous armoured chest securely bolted to the floor. There it was and very well sealed with a large armoured padlock. It must have taken a very strong team of dockers to load it onboard without the crew ever seeing it at the port of La Orotava.

Using every implement they could lay their hands on, the three mutineers eventually burst the lock open. On lifting the heavy lid, they stood back in awe at what faced them. They could not believe it. This was truly an extraordinary sight. The chest was filled to the brim with such treasure as they, or indeed many others, had ever seen. They stood there in silence for some moments simply stunned at the spectacle before them.

Waterford Estuary, Ireland (Credit: IrelandXO.com)

The contents of the armoured chest included gold ingots, 270 bags of Spanish silver dollars, each one distinctly marked, 3 lbs of gold dust, an array of exotic jewellery and more gemstones than could ever have been imagined. Ironically, on the top of the hoard there were also some bags marked with the initials of Captain George Glass. These contained a large proportion of his accumulated gold wealth, which he was bringing home with him. The spectacle was so great that it made every one of them feel an air of both great excitement and fear. This was almost too overwhelming for the semi-literate and shoeless deckhands. Had they bitten off more than they could chew?

Once their euphoria had subsided, reality quickly took over and real panic began to set in. They had to decide immediately on what to do next. On resuming their voyage, they would soon be in view of any observers watching from the shores ahead. They could not risk detection. Somehow they had to find some way of quickly disappearing with their riches, leaving no evidence of their murders and mayhem. With little time to agree a detailed plan, as they were now anchored in a very busy shipping lane and passing vessels might be curious, they agreed that they would have to get ashore somewhere along the coastline that lay ahead. MacKinlie guessed that the coast was most likely that of Waterford or even Wexford, in the south-east corner of Ireland. They did not know that the imposing and heavily armed Duncannon Fort also lay directly ahead; if they did, they might well have turned around and sailed elsewhere. Constructed by Queen Elizabeth I in 1587 to combat any possible invasion of Ireland by the Spanish Armada, the fort was a significant military base and had commanding views not just of Waterford estuary and Wexford's coastline but even of the approaches from the Bristol Channel and England. This armed battlement would also have been known to the great Irish pirate queen, Gráinne Mhaol (Grace O'Malley), as she passed by on her way to Dalkey Harbour further up Ireland's east coast from her 1595 meeting with Queen Elizabeth I.

The mutineers now decided that they would have to abandon their ship. It was far too visible. They would instead attempt to row all the way to a safe landing place somewhere ahead of their position. Their hope was that in a smaller boat they would be less visible from shore as they approached land. At this time they were still anchored approximately seventeen miles from the coast, quite a distance for a heavily loaded small craft to cover. The four mutineers were already very tired and nursing various wounds, some more serious than others. Fortunately for them, there was a heavy morning mist drifting towards the Irish coastline.

It was now Tuesday, 3 December 1765. As quickly as they could, they set about launching the *Earl of Sandwich's* longboat over the side. They even succeeded in getting the help of the two terrified youngsters whose lives had been spared, so far. The twelve-year-old cabin boy, Benjamin Gallispey, and the Glass family's young servant boy, must have seen this as a sign that they would be safely rowed ashore by the mutineers and probably abandoned there. If all on board the longboat were lucky, they would soon find a safe sandy beach, rather than a dangerous rocky coastline, and somehow quickly make their escape.

Our mutineers were clearly not aware that gold is significantly heavier than lead. It took them far more time than expected to organise and prepare for their next challenge as dawn broke on that cold December morning. All hands were needed to load everything onto the longboat below. One by one, the very heavy bags of gold ingots, Spanish silver dollars, jewellery, gemstones and gold dust were carefully lowered over the side by rope, a painstakingly slow process. To make sure the boat was safely balanced, they spread the load as evenly as they could but still had to leave enough space for the mutineers to fit. As the hoard piled up in the small rowing boat, the mutineers were soon shocked by how low it was now sitting in the water. The weight, estimated to be over two tons, began to bring the boat dangerously close to sinking as water lapped over the gunwales. Luckily, the sea was relatively calm so far. Fearing that they could lose the lot, the mutineers were very reluctantly forced to throw some of the treasure overboard, just to lighten the load and keep them afloat. This treasure is probably still somewhere on the seabed below today. Fear was now overtaking them as the murderers plans for a quick and unseen escape began to unravel. It would soon be broad daylight.

In an effort to hide all the evidence of their mutiny, they finally returned below deck and as later reported, "knocked out the windows of the ballast-ports" in their attempt to allow the sea to pour in and sink the *Earl of Sandwich* as quickly as possible. The wilful sinking of a relatively large vessel is no easy task; it take's time, a commodity which they just did not have. These sturdy oak brigs were built to absorb the pounding of heavy seas and even to being beached and were not easily damaged. All the mutineers could do now was let the sea fill the hull and pull the entire ship below, where it might never again be found.

As they finally began to row away with their very rich cargo, leaving the brig behind them to sink without trace, the terrified twelve-year-old cabin boy, Benjamin Gallispey, who was a good swimmer, jumped overboard and swam after the departing crew. On reaching them, he desperately tried to pull himself on board. St Quinten, feeling sorry for the young lad, grabbed him by the collar in an attempt to haul the child over the stern. However, the other mutineers, not wanting to have any witnesses to their actions of the past twenty-four hours, even very young ones, screamed that if St Quinten did not release the cabin boy immediately, both would go in to the sea. The unfortunate youngster was cruelly beaten off with an oar. Still wearing his tight skull cap in the water, throwing it in the air, he was heard to scream "O Lord, have mercy on me," before he sank to the seabed below.

The four mutineers, P. MacKinlie, G. Gidley, A. Zekerman and R. St Quinten, raised their oars, set a steady rhythm and headed for the coast over seventeen miles away, abandoning the remaining young lad who had been taken on board in Tenerife by Captain George Glass. With the help of the early-morning mist blowing in from the sea, they were still just about out of sight of Duncannon Fort, high on the Hook Peninsula in County Wexford. They hoped to make it inland somewhere south of the fort and beyond sight of the law.

Seeing the mutineers rowing away, the stranded young lad left behind panicked, ran to the helm of the slowly sinking ship and somehow managed to turn it in the mutineers direction, towards the coastline. When the men looked around, to their horror, they saw that the *Earl of Sandwich* was making some progress towards them and still not sinking. In view of the savagery of the past few hours, this was becoming a comedy of errors. If seen, the *Earl of Sandwich* would certainly attract attention and especially with a child at the wheel! The

Sixteenth century Duncannon Fort overlooking Waterford Estuary

murderers would never live to enjoy their precious haul. Cursing their bad luck, they very carefully turned around the longboat, constantly in fear of taking water on board. They were already suffering from exhaustion from the mayhem of the night, lack of sleep and their injuries. Now they were forced to head back to the still floating vessel to kill the young lad and try to speed up the sinking. As they approached the *Earl of Sandwich,* like an injured whale it listed and slowly rolled onto its side. In doing this, the young lad was seen to be thrown into the sea. As far as the crew were concerned, they had avoided a disaster and once more turned their rowing boat towards land.

The death toll, all in a period of less than twelve hours, had now reached the appalling number of eight. If stealing wine on board the *Earl of Sandwich* had seemed like a major crime earlier during their voyage, they now had no doubt whatsoever that their crimes would attract the ultimate punishment if caught.

The December morning remained cold and misty, and fortunately for the four mutineers, it still provided them with some cover from curious eyes. When they finally got close to the shore, they could see the wide mouth of the River Barrow flowing into the natural, wide opening of Waterford Harbour estuary straight ahead. Hook Head, in Wexford, was to their north, and Tramore Strand, in Waterford, to the far south. Before coming into possible view of Duncannon Fort, which was a fair distance in from Hook Head and located on the elevated headland above them, they rowed to Booley Bay, just before the approach to the fort. This is a beautiful but sparsely populated area on the coast of Wexford. A "booley" in Ireland is a local word for a small stone shelter used by farmers for protection when out herding their cattle. They were fortunate that at this hour, there was no sign of any early-morning herders in the area. This Wexford coastline was also a haven for pirates and privateers back in the early 1600s and continued to be so until Cromwell's arrival there in 1650. To some extent, the local population would have been used to foreigners coming in from the sea.

Through pure good fortune they found an ideal concealed sandy landing place, tucked below the fields above and hidden from view. Just beside it lay a similar but smaller beach, known today as Dollar Bay. Perhaps this got its name from some Spanish silver dollars which may have been found there later, or perhaps the mutineers spread out over both landing places as these beaches are just yards apart. Once their boat was beached, they wasted no time and immediately dragged ashore the massive two ton load of 251 of the 270 bags of silver dollars and other treasure. Although there are no large caves at this site, several very small hiding places were available between the rocks and in the soft sand above the high-tide mark. This heavy load was not easy to conceal. It must have taken quite some time to bury the large hoard. The remaining nineteen bags of silver dollars and booty they kept in their boat. Although this appeared to be a deserted area, they would have continued to worry that farmers working early that morning in the surrounding fields could spot them. Having already agreed to make no maps of their treasure's exact location in case any of them were captured, it appears that their plan was to return sometime later with a larger boat, divide the now hidden treasure between them and then go their separate ways as quickly as they could, away from Booley Bay and Ireland. At this moment, they had no way of knowing how they might do that or indeed how far they had to go to fully secure their escape. However, the nineteen bags of gold coins which they kept at this stage would be of great help.

Returning to their longboat, they pushed off again. Very soon the imposing star shaped, sandstone fort towered above them. Taking great care to skirt below it, unseen, under the cliffs at Duncannon, they took full advantage of the heavy damp mist that still clung to the coastline and had also drifted up the mouth of the estuary. Once clear of the fort, they continued rowing up the River Barrow for another ten miles. Coming around a sweeping bend in the river, they decided to pull up on the muddy flats at a place called Fisherstown. This was really just a cluster of houses rather than a town or village, and with few curious eyes around, the mutineers managed to remain unseen.

It was now time to part company with their row boat. Cursing and swearing, the exhausted foursome dragged it up through the mud and concealed it deep in the undergrowth

Booley Bay in County Wexford, Ireland

along the river bank. Once kept as domestic pets in Ireland, only a curious long-legged crane perched on one leg nearby showed any interest. Their next decision was to bury six bags of their treasure here, again, just above the high-water mark, and keep the remaining thirteen bags for whatever expenses might lie ahead. With no maps or local knowledge, how they expected ever to remember where they had just hidden this loot is a mystery. But they had no other choice as they were now totally exhausted, hungry, disorientated, injured and generally in very poor shape. They called to one of the few local farmhouses, and as they were not short of money, they succeeded in hiring four horses. These they paid for with Spanish silver dollars, not something the farmer would easily forget. Once they had something to eat and were saddled up, they asked the farmer for directions and set out for the nearby town of Ross (today called New Ross). This was just nine miles away, and if they had enough energy, they could have walked it, but their heavy bags ruled that out. From Ross they would then have to figure out how they might make it all the way to Dublin without detection.

As the sun rose higher in the sky, the mist and cold of this December morning of 1765 continued. It was time to get going. Turning north and away from the River Barrow, they rode carefully for two miles further along the narrow country lanes to a place called Ballybrazil, another small townland, which today borders JFK Memorial Park. Now without sleep for almost two days, all of the mayhem on board the *Earl of Sandwich* had caught up with them. Still in soaking-wet clothes as it had remained damp since they first set foot ashore, they urgently needed to get some proper rest. No doubt their clearly visible injuries, English and German accents, and overall scruffy weather-beaten appearance would have raised alarm bells for anybody who happened to see them in this quiet rural neighbourhood. So they rode on.

The port city of Ross on the banks of the River Barrow, was now only seven miles away. Within the hour they were at last approaching the town and in sight of a warm tavern with the promise of food and sleep. This busy inland river port was well used to foreign strangers. Some years later, many victims of the Great Famine of 1845–9 emigrated by ship from here to America. Many of the stronger ones who survived that sad journey headed to a harsh life and the blistering summer heat of Savannah, Georgia. Tragically, having survived both the Great Famine at home and the terrible Atlantic crossing to America, many of these Wexford emigrants would die lonely deaths in Savannah in the tragic yellow fever epidemic of 1854.

Once the mutineers found lodgings in Ross, showing poor judgement yet again, it was agreed that they would leave the drunkard MacKinlie in the tavern to guard their riches. The others then headed back to Fisherstown to fetch the six bags of silver dollars they had hidden there. Before departing, they warned MacKinlie to be careful, to stay sober, and most of all not to attract attention. They also asked the landlady if she could set the fire in their room so that they could dry some of their soaking-wet clothes and gave her a very valuable necklace and some gold earrings in compensation. Of course, she immediately showed the valuables to all her clientele.

These mutineers never did anything the easy way. Some hours later, having successfully retraced their steps and somehow located the bags of coins buried on the muddy banks of the river, they arrived back at the tavern in Ross. On entering the cosy smoke-filled building, the raucous party atmosphere must have felt like heaven for the three murderers as they nervously scanned the room in search of their alcoholic bosun. To their absolute horror, in the middle of all the celebrations, there stood MacKinlie. The deep and weeping wound in his arm was clear for all to see, but it didn't seem to dampen his spirits. He was probably partly anaesthetised by this time and felt no pain. Now surrounded by the locals, he had made far too many new friends as he paid for more and more beer with silver coins. Stupidly, MacKinlie had also boasted to his recently acquired tavern friends about his newfound wealth, making all four of the mutineers even greater targets for whatever crooks might be in this busy river port. Even without this foolish behaviour, wealthy drunken strangers in this remote area would have attracted attention anyway, both good and bad. Yet again, MacKinlie was a festering liability!

Of this incident, a report in the *Freeman's Journal* in December 1765 stated:

> By a man who came last night from Ross, we learn that four sailors came there on Wednesday, and they were going to Dublin. They had several bags of dollars, numbered and made up after the Spanish method for the use of merchants. They were very prodigal of them at the Publick Houses, particularly to females. They gave a large gratuity to a guide, and after purchasing a case of pistols, set off in the morning for Dublin.

Eventually, following a long night of heavy drinking, they all retired to their warm and cosy room and were in an unconscious state within minutes. Their snoring would have told any who were interested that these mutineers could only be awakened by a Spanish canon going off beside their beds! They were easy targets. It is perhaps no surprise that only a few hours later, robbers quietly entered their rooms and without

Ship docked at the Port of Ross, County Wexford, Ireland

any trouble, helped themselves to some of the silver dollars, a rare currency in Ross in 1765.

Whoever was first to wake the following morning, Thursday, 5 December, rose the others. It was unlikely to have been Peter MacKinlie. The panic of the previous day quickly returned. On discovering the robbery, they dressed immediately in their freshly dried clothes, removed themselves from the tavern without being seen, and continued their journey to Dublin as quickly as they could.

The great advantage of having a ready supply of gold and silver was that it made it relatively easy for them to buy their three pistols, hire four horses and enlist the services of two mounted guides to lead them safely to their destination and return the horses. In all, they had now exchanged 1,200 Spanish silver dollars during their short stay in Ross, a fact clearly remembered by numerous locals after their departure as it was an extravagant sum and the town was much the better of it. Money talks. In spite of the fact that MacKinlie was Irish and should have at least known something of the general area, he seems to have had no idea where to go without a guide and was probably still too drunk to care.

Their raucous stay in Ross was noted by a local tradesman, as also reported in the *Freeman's Journal*:

> By a tanner from Ross this day, we are informed two of the men's faces already mentioned were much cut, and upon being asked how they came by such wounds, they said they came from Mexico and were met by a pirate, and that they received some wounds in defending their treasure. Three of the four are English and the fourth an Irishman.

Mexico was a stretch of their imagination and Dublin now lay about ninety miles to the north of their tavern in the port of Ross. As they were carrying nineteen heavy bags of gold ingots and silver coins once again, less the amount they had already merrily spent in Ross, it would have taken them at least three long days to reach the outskirts of Dublin. Of course, the duration of the journey would also depend on how much entertaining they did each night along the way, so it is likely to have taken a little longer, but no record remains of those details. One account from the period gives a real sense of conditions for travellers on that journey; "What a touch of the times we here get! No roads, only paths, and these, no doubt, in places, not safe against highwaymen." By this time, suspicions were widespread about these profligate and dangerous-looking characters with unusual accents who were galloping from town to town. In those days, word of mouth spread almost as quickly as it does today. With narrow roads and lanes and few ways of travelling unseen in a group of six horsemen, they were desperate to reach the big city as quickly as possible. Dublin would be the perfect hiding place for them.

7

Dublin Escape

Dublin at this time was one of Europe's largest cities. It was expanding in all directions. The Irish Parliament based in Dublin was determined to avoid having a fiscal surplus at the end of each year as they would have been forced to return this to London. So major construction projects, street widening, paving and lighting investments created a boom whenever these surplus funds were available. This was just such a time. The gradual development of the port and shipping facilities out in Dublin Bay added greatly to the level of heavy construction work and port transformation activities. Even in what was known as the "old city" area around Christ Church, the level of activity was frantic, with narrow streets crammed with large stage wagons, gigs, hackneys and horse-drawn drays, barrows of all shapes and sizes, hundreds of traders, hawkers, tanners, peddlers of every description, workshops and more. The spirit of Christmas was in the air too. Close by were Christ Church Cathedral and the famous New Music Hall in Fishamble Street. This hall was where George Frideric Handel's oratorio, the *Messiah*, was played for the first time at noon on 30 April 1742, twenty-three years before the four murderers were to search for shelter in the area. Imagine how out of place the four wretches must have felt in these surroundings. It is interesting to note, as Handel's rehearsals with the orchestras and enormous choirs were so popular, hundreds came every day in the hope of catching a glimpse of the composer. The ladies were requested not to wear hooped skirts and the men were asked to leave their swords at home in order to create more space for the spectators! In the highly unlikely event that they may have wished to, Peter MacKinlie and his three compatriots would most likely have been refused entry.

Arriving on horseback in the middle of all this activity on 6 December 1765, MacKinlie, Gidley, Zekerman and St Quinten must have looked a sorry sight. On the outskirts of Dublin, they finally parted company with their guides, returned the horses to them and paid for their services. Spanish silver dollars were again the currency. After more than four days in the saddle, with ragged, bloodstained clothes, visible injuries and weather-beaten faces, they still desperately needed to take cover from the authorities and rest. It was hard to believe that this was just over a week or so since they were sailing peacefully towards the Isles of Scilly. It could all have been so different. Their plan now was to lie low in this bustling city, let the dust settle, return at a later date to Booley Bay in Wexford to collect their buried treasure, and finally to catch a ship and escape back to England or beyond with their fortunes.

After searching for a few hours, the four men found themselves in Thomas Street in the heart of the city. This was the main thoroughfare at that time with an imposing tall watch-house at the junction of Watling Street. Our visitors would have been wary as they passed by as watch-houses were manned by guards to deter criminals, keep watch for fires and recover stolen goods. The general atmosphere of the area is reflected in the street names of Dog and Duck Yard, Crane Lane, Dirty Lane and Crilly's Yard, with the Corn Market nearby. Christ Church Cathedral towered overhead and also overlooked Dublin's Newgate Prison, which stood on the site opposite St Audoen's Church today. Moved in 1781 to Green Street, because of its miserable state and notorious reputation, the prison was eventually forced to close in 1860, but it was now an ominous reminder, for the new arrivals, of the long arm of the law. This edifice was once an entry gate to the city on the south side of the River Liffey. Known even today as the Liberties, the surrounding area was full of busy taverns, boarding houses, brothels and hotels, and most weren't too fussy about who their guests or clients were, as long as they could pay. Nearby also were the Quakers' meeting house, Dutch Church, French Church and Roman Chapels. It must have seemed like a perfect hiding place for the four murderers. Hoping that they could easily blend in to these busy surroundings to avoid unwanted attention, they quickly found accommodation. They chose an establishment known as The Black Bull. This is likely to be today's Bull and Castle Pub, directly opposite Christ Church Cathedral. In order to be less conspicuous, once rested, the purchase of new clothes was their next task. However, their general appearance, accents and facial injuries suffered during the events of the past week, were too obvious to go unnoticed by some.

While the fugitives were busy replacing their ragged clothing, the wider world was quickly closing in on them. It transpires that their rushed and clumsy attempts to scuttle the *Earl of Sandwich*, were only half-successful. Their panic had forced them to escape from their leaking ship far too quickly. As all mariners regarded that area of the Irish Sea as a particularly dangerous one, they paid particular attention to their surroundings as they approached the Irish coast and Waterford estuary. Any floating obstructions or hazards were noted and the information was quickly passed to the authorities for circulation to help prevent serious accidents at sea.

A letter from the authorities in Waterford to their counterparts in Dublin, dated Friday, 6 December 1765, at the time when the four murderers were arriving at the outskirts of Dublin, stated:

> Last Wednesday (Dec 4th) evening at six o'clock, came in Captain Honeywell from Newfoundland. About 4 leagues to the SW of the Tower he had like to have run foul of a large three-mast vessel. The weather was very hazy, which prevented his seeing her. Her top gallant yards were up, and she was so deep in the water, that he could only see her sails. She had no boat on board nor could a living creature be seen.

This report triggered an immediate reaction. If the mutineers had any inkling of the publicity their murderous vandalism had now generated, they might have altered their plans and not have rested in Dublin. Eight boats were immediately sent out to sea at Tramore to examine the wreck, but very rough seas turned them back that day. Over fifty pipes of wine – those casks containing 125 gallons each – had already been washed ashore. A Mr Gahan and a party of soldiers from Duncannon Fort had secured these. The number later increased to seventy. Over the following days the flotsam also included a number of capuchins (hooded cloaks worn by women), bonnets and other women's apparel. Were these Christmas gifts from Captain George Glass and his wife for family members back home? As a wealthy man returning for the festive season following so many years at sea, this is more than likely.

When the *Earl of Sandwich* rolled over, it created a serious shipping hazard, as it did not fully sink. This area was littered with shipwrecks over the years. The murderers would never have thought that the wooden hull would be clearly visible on the long and flat sandy beach of Tramore Strand. This was just a short distance south of where they had first landed at Booley Bay. Once the tide went out and the weather improved, the name on the stern of the brig was clear for all to see as it lay there like a beached whale just beyond the sand dunes. In that quiet location, it did not take the local authorities very long to figure out the full story. The bloodstains from the slaughter of Captain Cockeran and the talented George Glass were still visible both above and below the deck. As reported, a large amount of debris, cargo and pieces of the ship's structure continued to come in with every new tide. One very unfortunate report stated:

> "Lost to posterity [is] a manuscript, relative to the west coast of Africa, which Glass had been about to publish, and which he mentions in his work on the Canary Islands."

How the author knew what George Glass had on board is unknown. The manuscript referring to the west coast of Africa almost certainly would have included precise details of exactly where his Port Hillsborough project was to be established. It still remains a mystery today. Indeed, there is no record of this manuscript ever having been recovered along that Waterford coastline or elsewhere.

Another report in Lloyd's List, dated 17 December 1765, stated:

> The bay at the eastern third of the strand is all sandy and the tide is long approaching the shore and there flows

very little, and ships are therefore at a great distance involved in great and terrible breakers so that men are seldom saved.

A Flying Coach, at that time, was capable of travelling at eight miles per hour, if the road surfaces permitted. The news report of the wreckage of the *Earl of Sandwich* was now quickly making its way from Tramore and Waterford to the authorities in Dublin, as reported in *The Newgate Calendar*:

> An express was despatched by two gentlemen to the lords of the regency at Dublin, exhibiting the several causes of suspicion, and giving a particular description of the supposed delinquents. On board the wreck was found a sampler worked by Miss Glass, from which it appeared that a part of the work was done on her birthday, which afterwards proved to be the day preceding on which the murders were perpetrated; and this sampler proved a principal means of leading to a discovery of the guilt of these abominable villains.

The level of revulsion generated by the atrocities which took place on board the *Earl of Sandwich* can well be understood from the recovery of that unfinished sampler referred to in *The Newgate Calendar* report. Parents George and Isobell Glass, must have felt so proud on seeing their young daughter Catherine, on her eleventh birthday, applying her skills and making such a very special effort to finish her delicate embroidery before Christmas and the return home of the family. Her embroidered gift may well have been intended as a present for her seventy year-old grandfather, reverend John Glas, who now had lost three members of his extended family in this dreadful tragedy.

It later transpired that the mutineers had earlier asked their landlady, when they rested at Fisherstown, to sew up some bags so that they could carry the silver dollars and gold on their saddles on their journey on horseback. Each of these pieces of information that were passed to the authorities were now forming a grim picture of the entire escapade. The landlady later regaled all her friends with her stories of the jewellery and silver she received in payment for her services.

Yet again, MacKinlie proved to be a liability. He now made their situation even worse by exchanging Spanish silver dollars in Dublin with a local goldsmith in the Christ Church area to a value of £300, thinking that this would not attract attention! As soon as the exchange was made, MacKinlie quickly left the goldsmiths premises in order to disappear into the crowds on the street. Within moments of his departure, the goldsmith panicked. While delighted with the transaction, he realised that having such a quantity of Spanish silver dollars in his possession had now put him in the unfortunate position, at some stage, of being accused of receiving stolen goods. That made a sentence to the pillory, whipping, or a dreaded prison term, a distinct possibility. Immediately, he closed his shutters, locked the door, stepped outside and began a desperate search for MacKinlie to see where he might be residing. In the busy narrow streets, this was not an easy task but guessing that he was likely to be heading towards the hostelries around Winetavern Street, a short distance away, he quickly spotted the mutineer limping as he carried his bag of coins back to his nearby lodgings. Wasting no time, to both avoid trouble with the law and also in an attempt to keep his Spanish coins, he noted MacKinlie's address and immediately headed straight to the Watling Street Watch House to report the whereabouts of his silver dollars customer. By this time, the authorities had already widely circulated detailed descriptions of all four murderers and organised several search parties for them. The story had become one of national disgust. While the hull of the *Earl of Sandwich* slowly disintegrated with the tides and currents along Tramore strand, sadly, the bodies of the victims were not recovered.

The first mutineers to be identified and apprehended by the authorities in the Christ Church area were the seemingly naive St Quinten and the tall Dutchman Zekerman, who must not have been that difficult to identify. It seems that neither offered any resistance when arrested. Both were immediately transported to Newgate Prison, still one of the most dreaded places in Ireland at that time. As the two murderers lay in chains on a bed of dank straw in the cold granite prison building, hearing the bells of Christ Church ring on the hour must have felt like the final countdown of their remaining time on earth.

Somehow, the other two, MacKinlie and Gidley, managed to evade arrest for the moment. However, Richard St Quinten and Andrew Zekerman knew where MacKinlie was and following what was most likely some very aggressive questioning, both spilled the beans to their interrogators. Soon after, with the help of the address handed in to the Watch Tower by the goldsmith and the confessions of his colleagues, MacKinlie was easily located and arrested. Only the Englishman George Gidley, the cook, was now still at large. He was somewhat smarter than the others.

Guessing that he could too easily be traced in Dublin now that his three associates had been apprehended, Gidley decided to remove himself from the city altogether and head for the busy port of Cork on the south coast. Hiring a post chaise, a fast four-wheeled, closed-body carriage drawn by four horses and used by many who wanted to travel privately and quickly, he headed off. Paying for his passage back to England from Cork would not have been difficult and he had the money to do so. He could then return later once the dust had settled to collect the hidden treasure and perhaps even keep it all for himself as his fellow mutineers might never see daylight again. He made good progress as the post chaise and four horses was designed for both speed and privacy. On arrival at Castledermot in County Kildare, just fifty miles south of Dublin, they had to stop to water the horses and Gidley could stretch his legs. This was a mistake. Unlike the infamous English pirate Henry Every, some seventy years earlier, who somehow managed to disappear forever when the global manhunt for him was closing in, the long arm of the law was now much more efficient. Within no time, Gidley was traced, identified, arrested and placed in nearby Carlow Gaol. From there, he was quickly transported under heavy guard all the way back to Dublin's Newgate Prison. He would finally join his accomplices, who now lay chained in their cells where they could all together hear the hourly peals of the bells of Christ Church Cathedral.

One report stated that at the time of his arrest, unlike the others who had bought new clothes to help conceal their identities, Gidley was still wearing the bloodstained blue frock coat with its brass buttons belonging to the murdered Captain George Glass.

Both St Quentin, the youngest of the four mutineers, and his fellow mutineer Zekerman, had by now confessed to everything, including the murders for which they were responsible. They were also forced to disclose the details of where they had hidden the remaining gold coins and other treasure. Fearing that salvage hunters might already be searching the beaches between Booley Bay and Tramore Strand, instructions were immediately sent to the soldiers based at Duncannon Fort. As little time was lost in issuing

C A P T. G L A S.   vii
said persons should be taken, and required to give an account of themselves.

THOSE gentlemen arrived on the 8th, and having informed the said magistrate of their errand, he, with proper assistance, apprehended St. Quintin and Zekerman, who being examined separately, each confessed the murders, and other matters before related; and also, that since they arrived in Dublin, Gidley and M'Kinlie had sold to a goldsmith, dollars to the amount of 300 l. by which means M'Kinlie was apprehended; and intelligence got, that Gidley had set out in a post-chaise for Cork, in order to take shipping for England.

HAVING received an account of the dollars that were hid, the magistrate of Rofs dispatched back the two Gentlemen, with directions to the Collector of Rofs, and the commanding officer of the fort of Duncannon, to make search for the bags of dollars: In returning, they apprehended Gidley in his way to Cork, and had him committed to Carlow goal, where they found upon him 53 guineas, a moidore, and some silver.

ON the 13th they found 250 bags of dollars sealed up, and brought them to Rofs under a guard, and lodged them in the custom-house.

THERE were found in the possession of M'Kinlie, Zekerman, and St. Quintin, some toys, a few guineas, an ingot of gold, and a small parcel of gold dust.

ON Saturday, March 1, the four assassins were tried and found guilty; and on Monday the 3d, they were executed at Stephen's-green; Their bodies were brought back to New—

Details contained in the 1767 book, 'A short account of the life of George Glas

these instructions, most of the treasure was quickly recovered from its hiding places. But most does not necessarily mean all.

As recorded in *The Newgate Calendar;* "The sheriff of Ross took possession of the effects found in the wreck, and the bags of dollars that the villains had buried in the sand, and deposited the whole in the treasury of Dublin, for the benefit of the proprietors."

Another report identified a telling fact: "The murderers spent more than the money alleged to be missing from the treasure." Clearly a quantity of Glass's private means must also have been involved.

The shocking details of the murders of Captain George Glass, his wife and their eleven year-old daughter, as well as Captain William Cockeran and the two young cabin boys had by this time been widely reported. For generations, people in Dundee, Edinburgh and Dublin would remember these shocking murders. The enormous degree of public interest and revulsion was probably the reason that the murderers were not left to simply starve to death in their Newgate Prison cells as so often happened with prisoners who could not afford to pay for their own daily rations. Their executions were to be a far more public spectacle, both as a general warning for people as a whole and even for public enjoyment!

Just three months later, on 1 March 1766, the trial of the mutineers took place in Dublin. Such trials were usually quick ones. The mountain of damning evidence and the many witness reports were overwhelming. Details of the court case read like a gruesome and heartless crime novel.

This widespread sensational publicity caused huge crowds to converge on the court in Dublin for the trial, which was packed to capacity. Ireland's most widely read newspaper of the time, the *Freeman's Journal,* founded only a few years earlier in 1763, also headlined all the details of the shocking affair. To nobody's surprise, Peter MacKinlie, Andrew Zekerman, George Gidley and Richard St Quinten were all found guilty of murder. Quickly convicted, each one of them was immediately condemned to death. The convictions and their pending hangings also became both national and international news.

One of the reasons we know so much of this tragic story today can be traced to Richard St Quinten, the youngest of the murderers described several times as "a man of slow apprehension". Although he did make some attempt to rescue young Gallispey from the water as they abandoned the sinking *Earl of Sandwich* vessel, he was also the one who grabbed George Glass's sword as he lay haemorrhaging to death outside his cabin door and then ran the dying man through three times with the weapon. He was also the one who helped to throw young Charles Pinchent overboard. While locked up in Newgate Prison and contemplating his final punishment, St Quinten it appears became very religious. He began by asking for a visit from what he called the Methodists. As a result of his request, daily prison visits followed. He appears to have also believed that with enough repentance, forgiveness by the Lord was possible. Perhaps he was not after all "a man of slow apprehension". The night before the trial, he read the Epistle to the Romans, in tears much of the time. The next morning he declared, "My sins are all forgiven." He decided that telling the truth the next day in court was what he had to do, and he kept his word. Following his conviction and death sentence, on the Sunday evening, his Methodist visitor spent two hours with him in his prison cell, and he is said to have declared that he had never been so happy in his whole life.

Weather records of 1766 show that it was a bitterly cold and dry winter, with freezing temperatures most nights. Dark and damp granite prison cells were not a comfortable place to be. Early on the morning of Friday, 7 March, before being transported to the gallows, Richard St Quinten was permitted to spend a little time with his fellow murderer, Zekerman, and pointed out to him passages in the scriptures that he should read. He added, "I am ready to die as I know it is just that I should suffer." Of St Quinten his confessor stated: "Repentance towards God, and faith in Our Lord Jesus Christ are all the Scriptures make necessary. And these as far as could be judged from appearances, were found in Richard St Quinten."

Although he seemed ready to face the hangman, St Quinten made a final last-minute attempt to gain pardon by somehow arranging for a Mr William King, a well-known merchant in Hull, to deliver a glowing character reference to no less than the Lord Mayor of Dublin, Sir James Taylor. It appears that young St Quinten had served on board one of Mr William King's ships as a young man and impressed all with his diligence at that time. His request was not successful. He was still one of the two men who had thrown young Charles Pinchent overboard off the Isles of Scilly without mercy and three times ran Captain George Glass's own sword through his chest as the poor man lay bleeding to death from a fatal knife wound to his stomach. Nothing would ever change that.

Sooner or later we all sit down to a banquet of consequences.
ROBERT LOUIS STEVENSON

8

From Fatal Tree to Seaside Gallows

Seventeen years later in 1783, just before he became prime minister of Great Britain, Ireland's Lord Lieutenant, the Duke of Portland, ordered that future hangings take place within Newgate Prison in Dublin and not at public places where large crowds could assemble. There was a good reason for this. His order followed the public hanging in 1782 of a robber and well-known gang leader named Mr Patrick Dougherty. It was alleged that he and an accomplice attacked a Mr Thomas Moran and stole his watch, his seal, his keys, his pen knife and even his silver-buckled shoes. A wine porter by trade, Dougherty was suspected of also having carried out many other armed robberies in the Dublin Port area.

Following Dougherty's hanging, a large crowd of relatives and friends broke through the cordon surrounding the gallows. After snatching the corpse, they carried it all the way to the home of the terrified Mr Thomas Moran on Lower Ormond Quay. Having been the victim of the robbery, the corpse snatchers viewed him as the cause of the loss of their relative, Patrick Dougherty. No doubt Mr Thomas Moran was in fear of his life when confronted by the spectacle at his front door and he immediately sent word to the authorities to remove both the corpse and his cohorts. But that was not the end of the affair. When the authorities eventually arrived and retrieved the body, they quickly brought it to Trinity College

Dublin, a short distance away, in the hope of delivering it to the college dissectors. However, on hearing the commotion, the porters at the Front Gate of the University slammed the heavy oak doors shut before they could gain entry. Avoiding dissection, the body of Dougherty was eventually returned to his relatives for burial.

This major disturbance created widespread revulsion and frightened the respectable neighbours living on Lower Ormond Quay. The Lord Lieutenant was not impressed with this carry on and made some changes. He declared that all future hangings would take place within the secure walls of Newgate Prison in order to avoid these unwelcome disturbances. Mr Patrick Dougherty, therefore, has the distinction of being the last person to be hanged outside the prison walls enclosure.

The scale of hangings in the 18th century is shocking to us today. In the fifteen years between 1780 and 1795, a total of 244 people were hanged. Now it was the turn of MacKinlie, Zekerman, Gidley, and St Quinten to receive their punishment. Early on the morning of 7 March 1766, following a sleepless night in their freezing damp cells, the four men were dragged in chains and loaded on board a black high sided horse and cart. The convicts were then escorted under a much larger than usual mounted military guard through the huge crowds that had already lined the streets, reflecting the level of both national and international publicity and the revulsion which the tragic case had generated over the previous three months. Spectators would often throw rubbish or worse at the unfortunates on their final journey. Military guards were provided, as on this occasion, for particularly dangerous criminals and sometimes numbered as many as fifty or sixty. The authorities feared that members of gangs might attempt to free their accomplices along the way or that members of the public might even attempt to release their relatives. The horse-drawn cart continued the journey down the steep hill from Christ Church Cathedral and past the courtyard of Dublin Castle and on towards Grafton Street. The place of execution was known to all as the Fatal Tree. It was located some distance south of what is today St Stephen's Green beyond Kildare Street and Merrion Row and a short journey further south towards Ballsbridge. The black cart spectacle continued to wind its way slowly on past the stables at the rear of the large homes beyond the Green.

As the crowds grew larger and the military escort attracted even more attention, the journey was almost over. The buildings had now become sparser as little development had yet taken place this far south of the city centre. With open

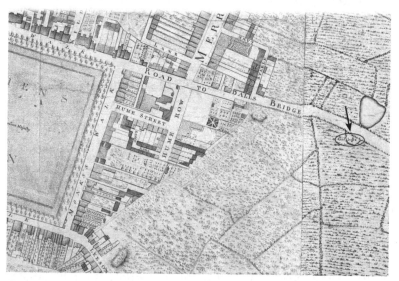

Stephen's Green area and the Fatal Tree Gallows – Bernard Scalé 1773 (Courtesy of the National Library of Ireland)

fields approaching on both sides of the road, the condemned men on board the cart would have known that they were nearing their final stop. In this peaceful farmland area, the gallows appeared ahead, overlooking a small, water-filled disused quarry on the far side of the road. The location was a perfect one for such large gatherings as on this occasion. The exact position of the gallows is clearly marked on the 1766 map of cartographer Bernard Scalé. The location is today buried below office and residential buildings and it is probably best that the occupants of the site are not made aware of this!

The horse and cart slowly pulled into the field on the right, where crowds had already gathered around the Fatal Tree. At this point, they all pushed forward in order to get a better view. The regulars who arrived earlier had their chairs and ladders in place for some time. Some even brought bread and cheese to feed their children during what could be a long day.

As the crimes of these particular murderers were so vicious and involved the cruel death of no less than eight people, including a woman and her young child, tempers flared and the crowds again pushed and shoved as the cart approached the powerful trunk of the tall Fatal Tree. With several hangings taking place every month in Dublin during the period, for some members of the public, it was a common spectacle to be enjoyed and even seen as amusement.

This was the month of March, 1766. The British government had just passed the Declaratory Acts confirming their "free and total" legislative power over the colonies. A very cold and dry winter was now followed by a cold spring. The scene in Dublin was not one for rejoicing as the predetermined fate of the accused murderers had finally

arrived. That happy scene of the Glass family boarding the
Earl of Sandwich on a warm 1765 November day in Tenerife
as they headed home for Christmas was now a lifetime away.

The more widely recognised execution gallows involving
an overhead beam and suspended noose and trapdoor
release contraption was a Victorian creation of almost fifty
years later. At this time, the branch of a sturdy tree was still
all that was required. Appropriately, the word "gallows" is
thought to derive from a Germanic word meaning "tree
branch". Such was the fate of the four condemned men
here as they reached the trunk of Dublin's Fatal Tree, its
leafless branches just set to awaken following the long
winter months. The criminals remained manacled and
shivering in the high sided black cart. The military escort
now struggled to keep the crowds back as their jeering grew
louder and louder. Wearing a mask to avoid later retribution,
as the hangman climbed on to the cart, the level of jeering
increased even further but soon an eerie silence reflected
the disgust of all towards the deeds of these criminals. The
murder of a woman and her child was detested by all and
this was no ordinary crime. The sentence was read aloud
for all to hear. Raising his voice and standing close by,
the clergyman offered some last-minute consolation. The
condemned man's hands were unshackled and then bound
tightly by rope behind his back as the hangman placed the
black hood over his head. Gripping the noose suspended
from the Fatal Tree above, he tightened it carefully around
the criminal's neck as he led him to the open end of the
high cart. Waiting just a few feet away for their turn, the
other condemned men would just have to watch or, most
likely, keep their eyes tightly closed. While death was usually

swift, that was not always the case. Once completed, the hangman took the belongings from the corpse, as these were then deemed to be his property and part payment for his services. Sometimes the dead man's family rushed forward to claim these often resulting in a serious skirmish.

Zekerman was the first of the four mutineers to be hooded. Surprisingly, he showed no signs whatsoever of either remorse or fear. If St Quinten's earlier reading of passages in the scriptures to him in his prison cell caused him to repent, we will never know. As a taller and heavier man than the others, Zekerman's end would have come quicker. When pushed off the cart, his greater weight would cause his spinal cord to snap almost instantly at the end of the rope; major blood vessels would quickly burst and the result would be immediate unconsciousness and death. Many in the crowd were familiar with the gruesome spectacle, and an expectant hush of anticipation rippled across the site as the final moment for Zekerman arrived. In total silence, the hangman reached up to ensure that the noose was secure around the taller man's neck.

THE NEWGATE CALENDAR
PREFACED TO THE 1780 EDITION

"With regard to the murderers, and persons convicted of unnatural crimes, we cannot think of altering the present mode of punishment. 'Him that sheddeth man's blood, by man shall his blood be shed:' as to the other wretches, it is highly to be lamented that their deaths cannot be aggravated by every species of torment!"

Once the nearby clergyman's "amen" was said, the hangman's push off the cart in to oblivion allowed gravity to complete the strangulation beneath the Fatal Tree. This was quickly followed by a loud cheer. When the moment came for St Quinten to be hooded, the clergyman prayed loudly with him in the hope that he would soon find favour with God. Just before the executioner took over, the young man was heard by many to declare "I know it, I know it." The sequence leading to death for this lighter man was different. As the rope found its length and his neck quickly stretched,

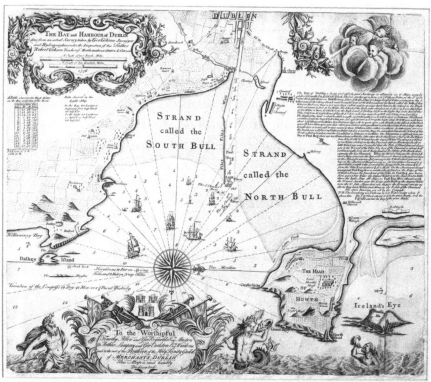

Bay & Harbour of Dublin 1756 with oak piles at the estuary
(Credit: Dublin Port Archive)

he would not have died immediately as the heavier man did. Over an agonising period of perhaps several minutes, the blood-flow to his brain was gradually cut off, rendering him unconscious till dead. If the drop off the cart was miscalculated by the hangman, those minutes could be a much longer period. On some occasions, family members would rush forward to jerk down the unfortunate culprit in order to speed up his death. Watching the twitching body of the victim would for some have added to the gruesome occasion.

When the hangman's noose had completed its job and the cheering from the assembled crowds had subsided, the corpses of the four convicted men were tossed unceremoniously into the horse-drawn cart. MacKinlie and Zekerman, Gidley and St Quinten, were slowly transported back to Newgate Prison. By then, the crowds had already lost interest. The large military guard was no longer necessary and it, too, disbanded. That journey of several miles back up the hill to Newgate Prison could well have been to a very different location. Surgeons, including those in Dublin, required a constant supply of cadavers for dissection and the anatomists in nearby Trinity College were close by. Dublin was renowned worldwide as centre for surgery and while the Royal College of Surgeons in Ireland was not granted its Charter for another eighteen years, in 1784, its predecessor, the Barber-Surgeons' Guild, dates back to medieval times. The demand for cadavers depended greatly on the supply of the hangman's trade. However, the bodies of these mutineers were spared this alternative outcome and for the moment they remained intact.

In a further macabre and unusual twist, the four corpses were not to be buried within the prison walls in unmarked graves. Soon after, they were again loaded back into the execution cart and transported from the prison to two adjacent locations at the mouth of the River Liffey. Each corpse was first bound in a shroud, coated in tar and wrapped in chains and iron bands, almost like a mummy. The metal hoops were secured tightly around each corpse. In this way, they were to be displayed hanging on tall oak piles at the water's edge, two at Poolbeg on the north side of the estuary of the River Liffey and two at the Pigeon House on the south side. These oak piles, more or less, marked the location where today are the North Bull Wall and the South Bull Wall, as described in the Epilogue. As a very busy but treacherous shipping channel, crews slowly navigating their way through the sand bars and mud flats on their way to and from the centre of the city, could not avoid seeing the gruesome spectacle of the four murderers, dangling in the wind, bound tightly and hanging by iron rings, not unlike sights of a torture scene during the Spanish Inquisition. It was certainly a serious deterrent to mutiny and murder for all to see. This was precisely the intention.

Although today's South Bull Wall, paved with granite hewn from Dalkey's quarries, was not fully completed till 1795, as an escape from Dublin's polluting smoke, open drains, litter and crowded city surroundings, this seashore location was a popular leisure area for all, especially for residents of the nearby small and ancient village of Ringsend. Recognised as a great fishing location as far back as the fifteenth century, the village was renowned for the delicacy of ray and was even known by some as Raytown. This was all a short stroll from the city centre.

The fresh sea air coming in off Dublin Bay was a great attraction. Not surprisingly, members of the public soon objected to the authorities about the gruesome sights facing them as they strolled along the seafront. The unsightly images and odours of the four mummified murderers were not what those taking the air wanted to either see or breathe. Eventually the stench from the decaying bodies on their oak piles above the high-tide mark became too much. Many sent their complaints to the *Freeman's Journal.* To make matters even worse, the bodies of MacKinlie and Gidley began to slip through their supporting iron hoops, creating an even more upsetting spectacle.

While the bodies of Zekerman and St Quinten remained secured to their oak piles for some time on the north side of the river, eventually their two bodies were taken down, much to the relief of visitors to this scenic area. They were then buried close by at the low-tide mark, and finally justice was served to this pair, "lying face down for all eternity dwelling on their damnable contrivances". The other two, MacKinlie and Gidley, were not granted this face-down muddy version of a burial. Responding to public complaints, they too were taken down but the authorities made different arrangements for them. It would seem that the extensive and gruesome reports in the papers of the mutineers cruelty, both at home and abroad, still lingered in the minds of the authorities, and so the two encased bodies were transported slowly by horse and cart south along the road that led from Ringsend, out through Blackrock, the small village of Dún Laoghaire, past Bullock Castle, and finally beyond the Queens Hotel and what remained of the seven castles of the Viking town of Dalkey. This part of their journey came to an end at what was still known then as Dalkey Harbour. This was over one hundred years before Coliemore Harbour was constructed later in

1868. The coastline referred to as Dalkey Harbour was full of small rocky and sandy inlets where boats had been launched and moored for many, many centuries.

One at a time, as they were now in a delicate state, the two corpses were carefully lowered in to a clinker row boat and then ferried a short distance across Dalkey Sound, not to nearby Dalkey Island, but beyond that to the jagged outcrop known for centuries as the Muglins Rock and where thirteen ships and their crews are known to have perished. Stronger iron bands were made to secure their decaying load. A specially constructed tall gibbet had already been erected there. Slowly, the two encased bodies were hauled up and secured from fixings on the crossbeam. Swinging loosely in the wind for all passing shipping crews to see and take heed of, they were a sorry sight. Apart from visiting gulls, terns and harbour seals, there was nothing else on the Muglins Rock to keep MacKinlie and Gidley company. The tall gibbet was also clearly visible for some time to members of the public as they walked along the scenic and sedate Dalkey coastline.

The shrouded bodies and the wooden overhead gibbet remained in place till the weather eventually took its toll and their remains decayed into oblivion. Just beyond the Muglins, where the water is over 50ft deep, the iron hoops and chains that secured the corpses of MacKinlie and Gidley may still be somewhere in the water below those granite rocks today! And so, finally, MacKinlie and Gidley, Zekerman and St Quinten ended up in irons on the seabed. Fortunately they were also some distance from their innocent victims somewhere out there in the Irish Sea – and a great, great distance from Port Hillsborough.

A report on 26 August 1766 in The *Freeman's Journal* gives an insight to the aftermath of grounding of the *Earl of Sandwich* and its demise:

> A part of the stolen goods were later recovered and the perpetrators were hanged and their bodies displayed on the Muglins Rock, off Dalkey Island. The ship was auctioned at the Customs House, Waterford, on 27 August 1766; To be sold by public cant, on the Customs-House quay at Waterford, on Monday the 15th day of September next, one hundred and sixty-three pipes, hogsheads and quarter casks of choice wines, of the growth of the Canary Islands, some raw silk and broad cloth, saved out of the wreck, *Earl of Sandwich*, stranded at Tramore, in the harbour of Waterford. The cant to begin at eleven o'clock in the morning and to continue until all are sold.

A Mr John Rogers of Tramore was said to have made a salvage claim six months later, on 23 February 1767, for the remaining 1,200 dollars that were found on board.

It has been a fascinating journey exploring the connections between the Muglins in Dalkey and Captain George Glass, his extraordinary life and tragic end, his adventures in West Africa and the Canaries, whaling, slavery, privateering and even rope-making.

But this eventful story still leaves us with some unanswered questions ....

John Glas and family grave in Howff Cemetery, Dundee, Scotland

PART THREE

PORT HILLSBOROUGH RIDDLE

"If you can't get rid of the family skeleton
You might as well make it dance"

GEORGE BERNARD SHAW

9

Scholars Differ

Just as they sometimes do in the movies, we are now digressing from this intriguing adventure tale to a behind-the-scenes look at how widely publicised stories such as this one can sometimes make a far greater impact than expected. Certainly, George Glass and his family could never have envisioned this to be possible. Even if it occurred over 250 years ago, a single event can ripple through the years and tickle the imagination for generations.

Do be warned: the tale has ended. But if you are interested, this now becomes a Sherlock Holmes-style attempt to look deeper into the journey travelled and how others may have gained from it, which I hope you may find interesting in Epilogue 1.

One part of this George Glass saga still remains unresolved. This has intrigued scholars, researchers and adventurers for over 200 years. The unanswered question is, where exactly was Port Hillsborough located?

For those with a great deal of patience, an academic document entitled *Memoria Digital de Canarias*, written mostly in French but with smatterings of Spanish and English, gives a great insight into the theories on the exact location of George Glass's mysterious harbour. I thank historian David Kelly for bringing this to my attention. Because Glass clearly did not want his discovery to be stolen by others, he created all kinds of red herrings as to its exact location, and the confusion that has resulted from this remains today.

Some clues – but again they may have been intended to conceal the true details – suggest that Port Hillsborough lies within a twenty-four hour voyage of the Canaries. This appears to be based mostly on two pieces of information. The first of these is an event that took place on 5 November 1764. That was when George Glass, following an attack by natives, was forced to leave the Port Hillsborough location and head for the Canaries to buy emergency food supplies and a larger boat. This voyage is reputed to have taken twenty-four hours, a key to where it might be located. The second possible clue came four months later, in March 1765, when Isobell Glass was also forced to flee from Port Hillsborough in search of her husband and also ended up safely back in Tenerife. That journey, too, is reputed to have taken twenty-four hours. If that was true, then the location of the port has to be somewhere nearby, on the coast of Morocco. The names of some possible locations along that coastline facing Tenerife have even been put forward over the years by many academics and historians and appear in *Memoria Digital de Canarias*. These include Assaka, not far from Marrakesh, and Santa Cruz de Mar Pequena on the southern end of the Moroccan coast. The names Gueder Regeala, Puerto Consado also appear on numerous occasions in later investigations. Two very interesting maps also appear in *Anuario des Estudios Atlanticos*, a cultural periodical with a special focus on the Canary Islands, suggesting possible locations at "le dunes de Tigidit". Both certainly look very attractive as easily defended potential ports. Certainly, these would all make sense if we stick to the "fact" that Port Hillsborough was within a twenty-four hour voyage from Tenerife.

It is usually unwise to go against the conclusions of learned historians and academics. On this occasion, I am going to do just that. The intrigue of George Glass's story is that his secret has still evaded researchers. He was very, very, clever at concealing his discovery. Who really knows how long those voyages took George and Isobell Glass to return to the Canaries from Port Hillsborough? We only have the secretive captain's word for that. Recorded statements that the discovery was within a twenty-four hour sailing distance from Tenerife simply could not be true. A voyage to reach only the nearest point of Africa is a journey of over two hundred miles. Sailing at a respectable six miles per hour, it would take almost thirty-four hours to just reach the coast. A spot that close and directly opposite the Canaries would already be well known to all. Any experienced navigator would have easily found that location.

George Glass worked too hard to risk telling the world exactly where he was about to make his fortune. The true location lay elsewhere and the real story points to an entirely different part of that coastline. Having "lived" and enjoyed almost every moment of George Glass's extraordinary life and adventures during my many months of research in Dublin, Dundee, Edinburgh and the Canaries, here are the crucial details that have put me on this totally different track:

- Most of the possible sites where Port Hillsborough might have been located according to many over the years are in what today, is the general area of Agadir. Yes, that is a possibility were it not for what was happening there at that time. It is worth noting that in 1764, while George Glass, his wife and ten-year-old daughter were happily sailing together for Senegal, Agadir was virtually out of bounds to visitors. Sultan Sidi Mohammed Ben Abdallah was very concerned about the revolting tribes in the Agadir area and he set off a whole series of attacks on them to subdue any threats. To all intents and purposes, it was a war zone. His troops would have fiercely guarded that coastline at that time of revolution. For me, this is a very good reason why George Glass would not have been interested in risking the lives of either his family or crew in that area of the coastline opposite the Canaries. Rather he would have sailed by as he headed further south.

- I refer back to a much overlooked record that contains this nugget of information in *Lloyd's Register.* "On July 13th 1762, a consignment of two large boxes of baft or rough cloth were shipped from Amsterdam to a man by the name of George Glass at a location in Senegal." Glass had travelled this long stretch of coastline for several years, knew it better than most and already had secretly selected a safe place in Senegal to receive this shipment of baft cloth from Amsterdam. How was he able to do that without already having some base or contact there? In my view, this Senegal location was not a quick and somewhat lucky discovery by George Glass. My guess is that he was returning to a place he already knew very well and had already established its potential as a fortified port. Its position lying directly across from Cape Verd would add further to its attraction as a trading base. The Portuguese had successfully proven that many years earlier. This was a viable area for trade but not easy for others to discover, which made it all the more attractive to Glass.

- When George Glass eventually found a way to surreptitiously
  communicate with the Home Office in London from his
  prison cell in Tenerife, it was reported: "Among the Home
  Office records is a letter from 'Mr. George Glass,' dated
  Tenerife, 15 Dec. 1764, in which he reports his seizure
  and close confinement in the castle. He suggests that
  the Spaniards dreaded interference with the important
  fishery carried on by natives of the Canary Isles on the
  African coast between Capes Bojador and Blanco, and
  asked for his release as recorded in *Calendar Home Office
  Papers, 1760–5, par. 1631.* Senegal, Cape Bojador, Cape
  Blanco and Cape Verde featured frequently throughout
  the many voyages of George Glass. He does not mention
  ports much closer to the Canaries, and why should he, as
  they were not the focus of his attention? As the Senegal
  area much further south was a dangerous and mainly
  uncharted region, both on land and at sea along the very
  challenging Atlantic approaches, it is unlikely to have
  been "discovered" by others up to that point. But George
  Glass knew it better than most, even from his very early
  days as naval officer.

- *The Newgate Calendar,* in detailing executions in the 1700s,
  although not always totally accurate on details, states:
  "Between the river Senegal and Cape de Verd he (George
  Glass) discovered a commodious harbour, from which
  circumstance he entertained the reasonable expectation
  that very great commercial advantages would be derived."
  Again this gives a much clearer indication of the most likely
  location of Port Hillsborough and it being somewhere
  closer to Cape Verd and not just across from the Canary
  Islands.

- As highlighted, the following took place in 1764 in the House of Commons: "Mr Bacon presented to the House, according to Order, a Bill for laying certain Duties upon Gum Seneca and Gum Arabic, imported into or exported from Great Britain and for confining the exportation of Gum Seneca from Africa to Great Britain only": This bill clearly focuses on the important area of gum production, which happens to be in Senegal. It is highly likely that "Mr Bacon" was to benefit from this proposed monopoly, but most important of all, Bacon was the one who presented George Glass's claim on Port Hillsborough to the House, and more than likely he was a friend who was privy to the details of Glass's explorations. Once again, a location in Senegal is connected to George Glass and his plans.

All of the named locations in Senegal – Cape Bojador, Cape Blanco and Cape Verd – are a considerable distance from the coast of Morocco where it faces the Canary Islands. We know that the coastal strip between Cape Bojador and Cape Blanco was one of the richest fishing areas in this part of the Atlantic. The fact that George Glass was active there was the main reason he was seen as a serious threat to Spanish interests and paid a heavy price for his activities by ending up in irons in the dungeons of Santa Cruz Prison in the Canaries. Knowing his abilities, he would certainly have been of concern to them and to their valued resources if he was permitted to establish his base in the Senegal area.

For all the reasons outlined, this is why I have selected the most likely sheltered inlet of the Delta du Saloum in Senegal, almost opposite Cape Verd. Just south of the Dakar peninsula and not far from the sensitive Spanish fishing grounds of Cape Bojador and Cape Blanco was a location with enormous potential for development. The Delta is 1,000 miles south of the Canaries and a sailing time of at least two weeks, not twenty-four hours, was needed to reach Tenerife at that time! Did George Glass suggest that his discovery was within one day's sailing time from Tenerife? That would certainly have been an excellent ploy to keep anyone who might steal from him his very hard-won harbour site. Certainly, the many conflicting exchanges in *Memoria Digital de Canarias* prove that, in this regard, he was very successful.

And so, if some day you or a resident of Senegal have both the time and inclination to explore this challenge further and arrive at the location of the Port of Hillsborough with even more certainty, do please write your story and share the fun. Even George and I will applaud your efforts.

Voyage upon life's sea
To yourself be true
And, whatever your lot may be
Paddle your own canoe

SARAH BOLTON

There is one remaining task to complete, however, something that adds a whole new dimension to our story.

THE "TREASURE ISLAND"

The ink is dreadful, the heat delicious a fine going breeze in the palms
And from the other side of the house the endless angry splash
And roar of the Pacific on the reef

ROBERT LOUIS STEVENSON, WESTERN SAMOA, 1889

10

Harvesting Real-Life Dramas

Some suggest that the infamous eighteenth century kidnapping of young James Annesley and the much publicised trial
in Dublin in 1743 was the basis of Robert Louis Stevenson's
Kidnapped novel. We have a more convincing theory. Is it
conceivable that there might be some connection between
Robert Louis Stevenson, George Glass and the Muglins in
Dalkey?

To explore this possibility, we will first take a closer look
at the story of *Kidnapped* as it has now emerged that this novel
had for many years a secret to share. Written in July 1886 by
Robert Louis Stevenson, who we will refer to as RLS to save ink
from now on, it was always intended to be a children's story.
To explain what emerged in later years, we need to return to
Scotland to take a look at two real individuals who even today
generate both debate and disagreement in their homeland and
beyond. They are named Colin Campbell and James Stewart.

In 1752 Colin Campbell was the manager of three large
West Highland estates in Scotland. These estates were at that
time in the control of the government. The Campbell clan
was one of the most powerful in Scotland and in particular
in the area of Argyll, part of the Highlands. This vast coastal
area north and west of Glasgow includes a total of twenty-three
islands. The influence of the Campbell clan stretched from
Edinburgh to as far north as the Hebrides. The Campbells
fought for Scotland against the English at the Battle of

The Writers Museum Edinburgh – the home of the Robert Louis Stevensons collection

Bannockburn and later supported Robert the Bruce. In the seventeenth century, they greatly benefited and expanded their lands throughout Scotland. They are often reputed to have acquired these lands through guile, and for that reason are sometimes referred to by some as the "hated" Campbells. During the Jacobite rising of 1715, the Campbells once again supported the government side, and in 1745, when they were reported to have had an army of 5,000 men, they fought against the Jacobites yet again. Scotland in the early sixteenth century was broadly a Catholic country. However, the Church in Scotland broke away from the Church of Rome in 1560, when Calvinism took hold. And so, in the 1750s, a Dr Webster carried out a parish survey which concluded that 95.7 per cent of the Highlanders were by then Protestant. With a strong tradition of religious dissent, as Highlanders, the Campbells were sometimes referred to as those dour Presbyterians.

On the other hand, James Stewart came from a long line of Scots who supported the Catholic Jacobites. Further back, during the early Norman conquest, the Stewarts had acquired land in England and subsequently moved north to Scotland. Their vast estates there were in the East Lothian area, to the west of Edinburgh and on Scotland's west coast. In 1371, Robert Stewart was the first of the Stewart family to ascend to the throne of Scotland as King Robert II. Much later, the Jacobites led by the Stuarts won the Battle of Prestonpans and the Battle of Falkirk in 1746 but were defeated soon after in the Battle of Culloden in the same year. According to Scot Web:

> Charles Stewart of Ardsheal led the men of Clan Stewart of Appin during the rising of 1745, and many fell at the grim field of Culloden, having first gained glory by breaking the Redcoat ranks. Colin Campbell of Glenure, 'the Red Fox', was placed as government factor on the forfeited Stewart estates.

In the late seventeenth and early eighteenth centuries, the Stewarts believed that the Catholic James VII of Scotland (James II of England) and his descendants should be restored to the throne of Scotland and England.

And here is the reason why it is helpful to understand some of the family history of the Protestant Campbell and Catholic Stewart clans. Clearly, they were very much on different sides of Scotland's political and religious divides and had been for generations. This all now gives us a very different perspective on a crime that divided opinion in Scotland for the following two hundred years, and this continues today.

This true story is crucial to the next part of our journey.

An infamous 1752 murder took place in the coastal town area of Appin, which is in the West Highlands. This is the town mentioned above, where "Charles Stewart ... led the men of

Clan Stewart of Appin during the rising of 1745". Appin lies 129 miles west of Edinburgh, not far from where RLS was born. The nearby Castle Stalker was built by another Stewart in 1495, taken by a Campbell in 1620 and recaptured by the Stewarts in 1685. These families had form!

This was a tumultuous time in Scotland, when Bonnie Prince Charlie's Jacobite army, supported by the Stewarts, was defeated by the government army at Culloden in 1746. And so, when this murder took place six years later, on 14 May 1752, it caused quite a sensation. It was alleged that one morning, a forty-four-year-old man by the name of Colin Roy Campbell, while he rode on horseback through the Wood of Lettermore in Argyll, was suddenly shot in the back and killed. Some said the shot was fired by a sniper rather than during some sort of row or hold-up. It appears that he was actually on his way to carry out the eviction of some tenants. However, these were no ordinary tenants. They just happened to be the Stewarts of Appin. Once evicted, Campbell intended to replace them with relatives of his own, more Campbells. The politics of the time are clearly highlighted by both the surnames of the victim and that of the accused. The very long history of the different loyalties of these families made this a sensational news story. Some would see it as a Catholic–Protestant conflict. The Highlander James Stewart of the Glen was quickly arrested, convicted of murder and hanged without delay or plea. Others were later suspected of the crime, including Stewart's son, but the hanging took place so quickly that little could be done to reverse the outcome. There was widespread sympathy for the executed James Stewart and his family. It once again brought alive in a very fierce way many of the historic Stewart / Campbell family animosities.

Subsequent studies of the high-profile case show that the evidence of James Stewart's guilt was, at best, very thin. Not only did he have a strong alibi, but eleven of the fifteen jurors just happened to be members of the victim's extended Campbell family. Even the senior presiding judge in the case was a member of the victim's family! To this day, scholars and scientists who examined the details of the murder are convinced that James Stewart was completely innocent. All the sensational details of the crime and the past feuds were widely reported in Argyll, Dundee, Edinburgh and throughout Scotland and beyond. Indeed the many newspaper reports kept the story alive for generations.

Now consider the wonderful story of *Kidnapped*. Putting his new steel nib to paper, as quills had just recently become a thing of the past, in July 1886, Robert Louis Stevenson wrote this story as a novel for young boys, and it was first published in the magazine *Young Folks*. RLS was thirty-six years old at the time and was not yet sure if his stories would be popular.

Kidnapped tells the griping tale of a seventeen-year-old by the name of David Balfour who grew up in Edinburgh. Having lost his parents, he decided to leave home and visit his uncle Ebenezer Balfour, who was reputed to be very wealthy. To David's surprise, he gets a very cool welcome, is almost sent to his death by his uncle and is mystified by why his uncle hated David's father so much. The uncle brings him to visit a ship in Queensferry. On boarding, he is knocked unconscious, recovers later out at sea and is forced to become a cabin boy. When a stranger is brought on board, the crew plan to steal his money. David alerts the stranger, who just happens to be named Alan Beck Stewart. Together they fight off an attack by the crew. The ship sinks and Alan and David are separated.

Alan leaves a message for David to meet him at his family home in Appin. On his way there, he meets four horsemen, all Campbells. One of them is shot by a sniper, and Alan arrives just in time to save David. Fearing they will be blamed for the shooting, the pair escape to the home of a James Stewart and then go on the run. A Highland leader helps them. Alan, being a Catholic Jacobite, taunts David for being a Protestant Whig and they fall out for some time. Eventually David makes his way back to his Uncle Ebenezer, secures most of his inheritance and funds Alan Stewart's escape to France. They also discover that Uncle Ebenezer and David's father had a falling out over the woman who became David's mother. They eventually agreed that David's father could marry the woman in exchange for the family fortune. David then rides off into the sunset.

It has since transpired that RLS and his wife, Fanny, discovered records of the famous Appin trial of the murder of Colin Roy Campbell while they were doing some research in the Highlands. The document "The Trial of James Stewart in Aucharn in Duror of Appin, for Murder of Colin Campbell of Glenure, Esq.", was almost an outline for a gripping tale. This was exactly what a gifted writer needed to fuel his imagination. RLS is quoted as saying "Suddenly the story moved, David and Alan stepped out from the canvas, and I found I was in another world." It is now accepted, as he made no attempt to hide it, that RLS based *Kidnapped*, written in 1886, broadly on the 1752 murder in Appin. All the Appin case elements were there: Highlanders versus Lowlanders, Protestant Campbells and Catholic Stewarts, a sniper in the woods and the threat of injustice. Going back to records and newspaper coverage of an earlier and widely reported story was an excellent way of finding the key elements for the creation of a great novel, just as we have seen in these past pages. RLS and his wife had a keen eye for a great story.

We know that RLS wrote *Kidnapped* just five years before he again sat down to attempt to repeat his success with another novel. This time it was to be the wonderful story *Treasure Island*. His method for creating captivating and exciting tales was working very well for him. His ability to combine both history, real-life events and fiction on the back of great characters, was the key to his success.

As with *Kidnapped*, RLS wrote *Treasure Island* as another children's story. It worked well before, so why not repeat the process? *Treasure Island* was first serialised in the same magazine, *Young Folks*, on 1 October 1881. This went initially under the different title of *The Sea-Cook*. Having now had considerable success in his literary career, RLS was also learning how the publishing business worked and how to generate some real income from his work. This time he requested payment by the magazine in the amount of £2.10s per page of 450 words. He added almost apologetically: "That's not noble, is it?" As with *Kidnapped*, the full book was published shortly afterwards, in 1883, with its final title of *Treasure Island*.

Here, briefly, is an outline of the *Treasure Island* story, and for the last part of our own tale, it is as good a place to start as any.

It all begins in Bristol in a tavern called the Admiral Benbow. The owner's young son, Jim Hawkins, becomes friendly with a mysterious long-term resident named Captain Billy Bones. One day, the captain has a visitor and this is where the adventure really begins. The visitor, with a name designed to give any child the heebie-jeebies, was Black Dog. Very soon, Jim's father gets ill, and soon after, so does Captain Billy

Bones. Sadly Jim Hawkins's father dies. In the meantime, the ailing Captain Billy Bones tells young Jim that he has a map which leads to a hoard of treasure. A blind man then arrives at the tavern, speaks to the captain and shortly afterwards, Billy Bones too dies. By this stage, Captain Billy Bones had run up a debt to the tavern. Jim and his mother then make their way to his room and quickly find a chest. From this they take what money is owed to them, but Jim also removes a small packet. This packet contains a map. On inspection it shows where treasure is buried at a place called Skeleton Island. The treasure was hidden there by the greatly feared pirate, Captain Flint. Young Jim, in search of advice, approaches his father's doctor and his friend, and on hearing the boy's story, the three of them decide to organise an expedition to find the hidden treasure. They hire a crew under a mariner by the name of Long John Silver and set sail in their ship, the *Hispaniola.*

As the adventurers approach the Island, young Jim overhears a conversation. It seems that Long John Silver and his fellow mariners are planning to kill the three who hired them and steal the treasure. At this point, the crew go ashore with Long John Silver, leaving the captain and Jim behind. Jim then decides to follow them, gets ashore and hides away as best he can. While hiding, he is startled to find Ben Gunn, who was marooned there three years earlier. The ship's captain then abandons the *Hispaniola* and, fearing attack by Long John Silver and his mates onshore, takes cover in an abandoned fort with a few loyal crew members. This is where Jim Hawkins finds them. The next day, Long John Silver approaches the fort, waving a white flag in an effort to steal their map. A fight follows and some are killed. Next, Jim goes back to their ship, has a fierce fight with a pirate, kills him and manages to steer the *Hispaniola* to a sandy cove. It then gets a bit complicated. Jim goes back to the fort. Long John Silver has grabbed the map but still they all join forces to find the treasure. After digging up the chest, they discover it is empty. As the pirates then turn on Long John Silver, one of them falls dead from a gunshot fired from the jungle. The others all flee. Ben Gunn comes to the rescue, saving Long John Silver, Jim Hawkins and their friends. Ben Gunn reveals that he has already hidden the treasure in a cave. With the help of Long John Silver, they quickly recover the hoard, race back to the *Hispaniola* and set sail for America. As expected, Long John Silver disappears overnight with some of the treasure, but the others all live happily ever after.

It is a simple but captivating tale: the thought of a place where a fortune awaits, a few good people on a voyage, a new ship and a hastily hired crew, an overheard conversation of treachery, a group of hired hands who turn out to be desperate pirates and murderers, a ring leader who directed all the mayhem, the planning of a mutiny, sword fights and death. But in this case there is a happy conclusion. Each and every one of the elements of *Treasure Island* feature somewhere in our Muglins saga, with the exception only of the happy ending. As RLS was writing his story for the children who read *Young Folks* magazine, it is more than likely that he wanted to finish on an uplifting and inspiring note, just as he had done in *Kidnapped*.

Informed by the history and geography of our Muglins story, we can now compare what we know with the basic bones of *Treasure Island*. While writing my version of the Muglins story, I was very fortunate to receive a communication from a fellow Dubliner, David Kelly. He had already clearly identified the possible Robert Louis Stevenson connection to the tragic story

Whale oil lamp at 17 Heriot Row in Edinburgh, home of Robert Louis Stevenson

of George Glass and his family. When David Kelly published his wonderful book *Pirates of the Carraigín,* he first detailed some of the events described in this book. A lecturer in early Irish history and a gifted researcher, he also spotted the very strong similarities between our Muglins saga and *Treasure Island* and his discovery added a whole new dimension to it. Could this be the second story based on historical facts that inspired RLS to write another great classic? I, too, was intrigued by this possibility.

Is it reasonable to think that RLS was already very much aware of these Muglins details before he even put pen to paper?

RLS was born on 13 November 1850 in Edinburgh and later grew up on Heriot Row, a short walk from Queen Street. This was eighty-four years after the hangings of the mutineers at the "Fatal Tree" in Dublin. The son of lighthouse engineer, Thomas Stevenson, RLS came from a devout Presbyterian family just like Captain George Glass. Shortly after the family moved to Heriot Row, RLS, at the age of six, dictated to his mother *The History of Moses*, an extraordinary feat for a youngster of that age. George Glass was also noted to be an exceptionally bright student and showed promise from a very young age. As we recall, *The Newgate Calendar* gives a clear insight to George's abilities while still very young: "At a very early period, young Mr Glass afforded strong proof of an acute and penetrating understanding greatly beyond what could be reasonably expected at his tender years."

In June 1859, at just nine years old, RLS was taken by his parents on a holiday to Dundee, sixty miles north of Edinburgh, where George Glass had spent endless hours watching and dreaming as he enjoyed the spectacle of the ships coming and going throughout his youth. George Glass had also visited Edinburgh on numerous occasions with his father, Reverend John Glas. The age similarities between Glass and RLS are likely to have created a great deal of empathy between novelist and the reports of the character of George Glass, increasing the possibility that the highly publicised story of the *Earl Sandwich* tragedy was very well known to him and the characters easily understood.

Becoming a literary celebrity early in his life, RLS's first publication, in 1878, was entitled *An Inland Voyage* and was based on his travels by canoe from Antwerp to northern France. Throughout his relatively short life, RLS suffered from poor health, which meant that he was forced to do a great deal of his writing and research at home. In fact as a younger child, he is known to have envied others of his age who were allowed to play out of doors. As RLS became a successful writer, his earlier time indoors gave him a particular talent for research, but later it also greatly increased his enjoyment and passion for travel, and he spent summers with young artists and writers in France. Just as in the case of George Glass, from a very young age RLS showed enormous interest in exotic locations and the promise of adventure. The two certainly had a great deal in common, even if our hangings and Muglins events had taken place 115 years before RLS even put ink to the *Treasure Island* page.

RLS travelled the world more than most do even today, again, just as George Glass did in his day. Both also disappointed their fathers in later life. RLS's father wanted him to be a lighthouse engineer or a lawyer, both of which he tried and quit. Rev John Glas hoped his son George would enter the Church or at least adhere to the strict beliefs of the Glasites. In fact, both RLS and George later lost their religions entirely.

In December 1894, at the age of forty-four, RLS died of a cerebral haemorrhage and was buried on the summit of Mount Vaea on Upolu, Samoa, where he had purchased land some years earlier. Both RLS and George Glass had their lives cut short at a point when they were most successful. RLS lived just four years longer than Captain George Glass.

A news item in *The Dundee Courier* at the time of the murders on board the *Earl of Sandwich* gives a sense of the impact on the wider community of the mutiny: "In his day, few events at home or abroad created greater stir or provided more sensation throughout the country." RLS may well have read these exact words when doing his research; indeed, it would be surprising if he did not.

The only questions is, should we still give RLS the benefit of the doubt and just put his great novel down to a brilliant imagination, or did he cleverly take the plot from another real-life drama of an earlier time? Considering his very keen literary interest, could it be possible that RLS never heard of George Glass, the mutiny and murders and the treasure hidden in Booley Bay, all of which are on record even today in the archives of Scotland's newspapers?

We will give this possibility one final test.

To take another look at the slim possibility that he just might have known nothing of the story, we need to take a stroll around the streets where RLS and his family lived in Edinburgh and see if that might reveal something unexpected. The geography is fascinating.

To say that the Scottish capital of Edinburgh has been shaped by stone would be a great understatement. Sandstone is everywhere. Some of it has been blackened by industrial pollution. Some has been lovingly restored. The city was once known as Auld Reekie or Old Smokie, and the impact of the Industrial Revolution is still to be seen in many areas. Both Old Town and New Town are beautiful examples of high-quality construction over the centuries.

> *For we are very lucky with a lamp before the door*
> *and leerie stops to light it as he lights so many more*
> *and o before you hurry by with ladder and with light.*
> *O leerie see a little child and nod to him tonight!*
> BRASS PLATE AT 17 HERIOT ROW, EDINBURGH,
> THE HOME OF ROBERT LOUIS STEVENSON

Clearly the preferred building material of the city's masons, and available nearby, sandstone is relatively easy to both quarry and dress. It was also the stone of choice when it came to the construction of homes such as those along stately Howard Place and Heriot Row, just a stone's throw from the busy

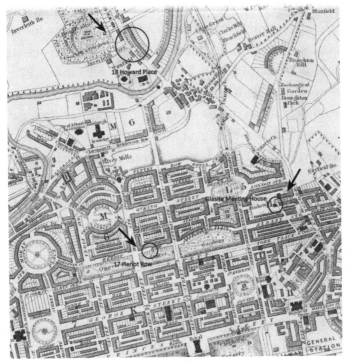

Edinburgh City map – featuring Stevenson family homes and
the nearby Glasite Meeting House, Albany Lane
Reproduced with the permission of the National Library of Scotland

Princes Street area. RLS was born at 18 Howard Place and grew up at nearby 17 Heriot Row. These impressive Stevenson family homes reveal some further coincidences and indicate how RLS might have known all about our tale of murder, mutiny and mayhem before he conceived the tale of *Treasure Island.*

RLS spent just the first six years of his life at 18 Howard Place. Although he was a sickly and only child of a respectable middle-class family, his first years were comfortable ones. Their solid sandstone home on the outskirts of the city is still typical of that affluent area today. It stands two stories over basement, with solid iron railings incorporating the traditional cast-iron pineapple symbol of welcome. As we know, his father, Thomas, and his mother, Margaret, both came from strong Church of Scotland family backgrounds, very much like that of George Glass. At this young age, RLS is unlikely yet to have known much about the local area but would have been aware of local religious meeting places. He might also have been influenced by his orthodox and somewhat terrifying nanny, Alison Cunningham, who believed strongly in the concept of hell and damnation. By the age of twelve, RLS had already visited France and Germany.

This is where our suspicions now turn to much more solid conclusions.

A short walk, just three streets away from Heriot Row, brings us to the corner of Albany Street and 33 Barony Street. In front of us we are struck by an imposing but rather sinister-looking two-storey, dark-brown sandstone building. At first glance, it looks abandoned and as if all the windows have been boarded up to keep squatters and daylight out. On closer inspection, clearly the material used to block the windows is in fact solid sandstone. This austere building was always supposed to look like this. Those inside the building were never supposed to be distracted by activities outside. The window recesses were never supposed to house glazed window frames. Only an elaborate and beautiful domed skylight window inside allowed daylight to shine through the ceiling in the upstairs gathering place after the services. And the reason is that this is in fact one of the original Glasite meeting houses! Almost intact and beautifully restored, today it still has some of the solid Glasite furniture of that era, the pulpit used during those long sermons and the pegs protruding from the walls for hanging the top hats of the 1700s. Some of the original pews, now used for gallery seating, still have children's initials carved in them, most likely to help pass the time during the long services. The upstairs dining room does have some windows and two attractive carved stone fireplaces. This would have been a very cold building in the 1700s and 1800s, but two blazing fires in the upstairs room would have warmed all the faithful. Some Glasite members still attended services here as late as 1989. Today it is an impressive gallery.

RLS lived just a hop, skip and a jump away from this building, which was constructed in the memory of Reverend John Glas, George Glass's father. Those blocked-up windows would have intrigued any child in the area and could not have gone unnoticed. It must have been a great curiosity to an inventive mind like that of RLS, and no doubt would have caught his attention as he strolled around his neighbourhood. The local population would certainly have been aware of those known as the Glasites, and considering that the mutiny and murders were so widely reported, the connection to this austere building would have made the tragedy almost a local story. Even today, that Glasite building at 33 Barony Street attracts curious visitors from far and wide.

It is now impossible not to believe that RLS, a gifted researcher, successful novelist, essayist, poet and travel writer did not know all about the link between the local Glasite meeting house, just down the road from where he lived, and the murders of no less than eight people, all connected to the Reverend John Glas and his son Captain George Glass. Those details were easy to access by any talented researcher. RLS must have known! Why not again grasp a real adventure and turn it into a great novel?

11

And So It All Ends at
the Muglins in Dalkey

Finally, let's go back to the beginning for another look at what has emerged over the pages. I can still clearly see the Muglins Rock from my bedroom window. The eerie moaning of the grey harbour seals at night, which reach the homes of all our neighbours throughout the year, must be exactly as they were in the period of our story. On dark winter nights, the flashing red Muglins light creates a great sense of awareness of the dangers of our rocky and sandy coastline and has saved many ships from damage and loss over the years. The strong south-east gales still lift enormous waves, which come crashing down over the entire length of this rocky outcrop. On calm summer evenings, this serious shipping hazard just beyond Dalkey Island, which acts as host to nesting terns and gulls, glows in the warm setting sun. Only one element has not survived nature's challenges over these last 250 years and that is the lonely sight of the gibbet that once supported the corpses of those callous pirate murderers, Peter MacKinlie and George Gidley.

In September 1875, a Royal Navy officer by the name of Vice Admiral Tarleton proposed that a warning light be placed on the Muglins, as by 1876, thirteen ships had already perished here with great loss of life. A Mr J. S. Sloan, engineer-in-chief of the Commissioners of Irish Lights and the renowned designer of the Galley Head Lighthouse in Cork, submitted his plans for a structure to be erected on the rock to warn ships. Three years later details of the conical stone beacon were agreed. Finally, in October 1880, this beacon was completed. It was initially painted white. Three years later a red band was painted around its waist. This is how it is today. It also marks forever the final resting place of two of those who murdered Captain George Glass, his family and eight people in total.

In preparing the foundations for the beacon, it is possible that the contractors would have discovered some of the iron hoops that bound the bodies of MacKinlie and Gidley as they dangled from the gibbet above in 1766.

For those who are interested in this significant landmark, originally it was designated as a beacon, but in 1979 it officially became a lighthouse. Following the trial and use of several methods of fuelling a flashing light, which must blink every five seconds, oil gas and carbide acetylene were used. In 2008, the old white warning light was changed to a red one. Today a solar panel powers the electric light, and it is now visible for approximately eleven nautical miles. My bedroom is nearer!

As a piece of local history, the pirate story has intrigued me and others for many years. Having now, with the help of so many, uncovered much of the saga that eventually followed the path of two of the four murderers to Dalkey and to their final and uncomfortable resting place, the story has turned out to be even more intriguing than ever expected.

For many, the locations and names of such places Dalkey, Dublin Bay and certainly the Muglins, will be new. The setting of the lonely gibbet on that rocky outcrop where two of the mutineers were finally displayed is also one overflowing with fascinating historical connections. The following pages will give some insight to these and given that we are recalling events of some centuries ago, the scale of many of the activities at the time would be difficult to repeat even today.

The history ....

EPILOGUE 2

THE HISTORY

I lived on a hilltop with the most beautiful view in the world,
I had only to open my eyes to see such pictures
as no painter could make for me.

GEORGE BERNARD SHAW ON DALKEY

12

There once was a place called Dalkey Harbour

As this story ended in a place called Dalkey, some insight to its fascinating history might help to give the saga a backdrop and a sense of place. A short skip through the centuries clearly shows that this quiet seaside town has had quite a tumultuous history.

If you ever happen to find yourself in the heritage town of Dalkey, just south of Dublin on Ireland's east coast, you will more than likely end up looking out to sea towards Dalkey Island, now uninhabited, although it was not always so. This twenty-two-acre rocky island lies just 1,000 ft offshore, beyond Coliemore Harbour and Dalkey's coastline, a safe landing area for seafarers for centuries. Dalkey Harbour is often incorrectly thought to be Coliemore Harbour, which is just down the road from Dalkey town. Many such references predate the actual construction of Coliemore Harbour, not completed till 1869. For the sake of clarity, any reference to Dalkey Harbour refers to Dalkey's coastline. Brennan's Quay, no longer visible, was one of several well-known landing places there in Dalkey Harbour. In his excellent 2015 "*A Historical Study of the Minor Harbours of the South-east of Ireland*", architect William Spratt-Murphy describes this area of the coastline in great detail. Included are water depths in the immediate area, which played a significant role in Dalkey's long history.

The local small scale lead and silver mining activities began close to Sorrento Point in 1752. Granite quarrying on Dalkey Hill, employed over 1,000 workers by 1823. Small rocky inlets along Dalkey's coastline were perfect for the shallow-bottomed clinker rowing boats that ferried goods ashore from larger ships anchored in nearby deep water. The goods were stored in Dalkey's castles and then transported north to the city of Dublin. The contractor for Coliemore Harbour's construction was John Cunningham, still a well-known name in Dalkey today. Plans for its two small harbour piers were drawn up by Dublin Port's renowned engineer, with the impressive name of Bindon Blood Stoney. The Dalkey area was altered significantly when large quantities of granite were removed from the shoreline and on land for major construction projects such as Dún Laoghaire's Harbour Piers, Dublin's South Bull Wall, the Liffey Quay walls, Kylemore Abbey in Connemara, Cork Cathedral, the Mall in London and even the Basilica of St John the Baptist in Canada's most easterly province of Newfoundland. Before the stone was removed, maps of the period show an indented shoreline, including several small, safe landing places. As there are depths of over fifty feet close to shore, much of the history of the area relates to heavy shipping at a time when the Dublin's Liffey was a sand-bound muddy river and Dublin Bay was littered with shipwrecks.

When the Vikings arrived in the eighth and ninth centuries, Dublin Bay's treacherous conditions did not pose a problem for their flat-bottomed long boats. According to Dublin Port Company, from records of insurance claims, the wrecks in the bay could number over 1,000! As most hulls were made of wood, little if anything remains on the seabed today. This explains why there was a morgue attached to what is now

The Club Pub on Coliemore Road in Dalkey town. Bodies washed ashore from shipwrecks and corpses arriving during the Great Famine of 1847 were taken care of there.

Dalkey's history dates back to the Stone Age (8700–2000 BC). Dalkey Island, referred to in some old sea charts as the island of St Benedict, was first occupied over 6,000 years ago. A microlith cutting stone found there in 2019 was also firmly dated by Ireland's National Museum to the early Irish Mesolithic period, often referred to as the Middle Stone Age (8,000–7,000 BC)

The Vikings arrival brought the creation of a slave-trading post on Dalkey Island. They traded with Chester, Chepstow, Gloucester and Bristol, and also with several European countries. In escaping from persecution in Norway in the ninth century, the Viking explorer, Ingolfur Arnarson, arrived in Iceland and landed near Reykjavik. With a serious shortage of females there, the Vikings returned to Ireland and

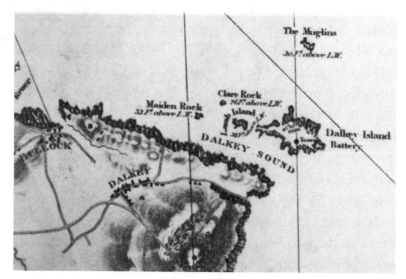

Dalkey Harbour before Coliemore Harbour construction – Alexander Nimmo Survey
Credit: National Library of Ireland

kidnapped women in order to address the problem. Legend has it that many of the Irish women, unlike many of the local Reykjavik population, could read and write, and are reputed to have made quite an impact on Iceland and on its history as a consequence.

While today the town of Dalkey is an upmarket residential area and popular tourist destination with a population of just over 6,300, a few highlights from its extraordinary past give an insight to its maritime significance.

From the eleventh century, St Begnet's granite church still stands roofless on Dalkey Island as evidence of the Island's early religious role. In 1804, when stone masons were employed to build the Martello tower on the island, to save them the trouble of rowing ashore at the end of each day, they fitted out the tiny church as living accommodation, added a fireplace where an alter once stood and enlarged the doorway and some of the windows. There is some evidence that an overhead cable linked the island to Sorrento Point so that essential supplies could be hauled over in bad weather.

In 1176 the Anglo-Norman Lord of Meath, Hugh de Lacy, granted this area, including Dalkey Island, to the See of Dublin, the jurisdiction of the bishop. This gift was confirmed by Prince John, King of England (1166–1216) and later by Pope Clement III. In 1399 the high constable of England, the Earl of Rutland, arrived with one hundred ships of war and sheltered in Dalkey's deep waters, confirming its importance as a safe place of anchorage.

Recognising the importance of the area, *Holinshed's Chronicles*, published between 1577 and 1587, stated, "Dalkee and Wickinlowe were among the chief haven towns of Ireland." In 1482, by grant from King Edward IV, Dalkey was

permitted to hold seven fairs each year, and if commanded
to do so could even raise two hundred men-at-arms. In 1488,
together with Meath, Louth and Kildare, Dalkey was included
as one of "the four obedient shires of the Pale", a fortified
area of safety and the base of continuing English rule in
Ireland. However, if your name just happens to be Byrne or
O'Toole, your ancestors were the likely reason for the local
fortifications, as these Wicklow tribes were a constant threat to
the Dalkey inhabitants and terrified the local community with
regular raids before retreating back to the nearby mountains.

In 1593 a historic meeting took place on the banks of
the River Thames at Greenwich Palace, downstream from
London. At the time England was fighting a battle against
the plague which had also spread to Ireland. The sixty-three-
year-old legendary Irish pirate queen, Gráinne Mhaol (Grace
O'Malley), with her long flowing grey locks, ruddy windswept
complexion and intimidating stature of over six feet,
audaciously sailed up the river and demanded an audience
with the sixty-year-old Queen Elizabeth I. Gráinne Mhaol had
a serious reason for risking her life. By contrast, the English
Queen was a small woman of just five feet and three inches
and appeared to be going bald. It was forbidden to outshine
the queen in any manner of dress or presentation and servants
who tried were usually punished. She must have been quite a
strange sight as she used Venetian ceruse – a lethal mixture
of vinegar and poisonous lead – as a skin-whitening powder.
This caused serious damage to both skin, eyebrows and hair
and would explain her apparent baldness. Being almost the
same age and both being able to converse in Latin might
explain why the queen and Gráinne Mhaol enjoyed each
other's company so much. It might also explain why the Irish

pirate queen was able to achieve her goal. Her son Tibbot-na-Long had earlier been implicated in an Irish rebellion against Her Majesty's occupying forces. Whatever bond was created between these two powerful women, it resulted in the Irish pirate queen securing her son's immediate release from prison. Celebrating her success, Gráinne Mhaol turned her ship around, safely headed back down the Thames to the English Channel and sailed north-west across the Irish Sea to arrive at Dalkey Harbour.

With the plague causing havoc in Britain and on the continent, it was also reported that "a remarkable plague" in the city of Dublin forced thousands of its citizens to take refuge in the "health abiding", nearby seaside place of Dalkey. Many of those fleeing from the disease are reputed to have lived in tents on Dalkey Island for the duration. This was again repeated during the later 1704–6 plague.

On 15 April 1599, Robert Devereux, the Second Earl of Essex, having been appointed Lord Lieutenant, arrived in Dalkey Harbour. Just imagine the sight. With one of the largest armies ever seen in Ireland – 20,000 foot soldiers and 5,000 horses on board – he was instructed by Queen Elizabeth I to oppose Hugh O'Neill, Earl of Tyrone. At that time O'Neill was recognised as the strongest threat to English authority in Ireland. The queen's clear instruction to young Devereux was to "subdue this restless island once and for all". No ambiguity there!

Being one of Her Majesty's favourites, much was expected of him. Having worked hard on charming the queen over the years, this was his reward. The investment in this huge army and all the necessary equipment involved must have strained even her finances, but it reflected her confidence in his abilities and also her fear of the threat posed by the Earl of Tyrone.

Within just five months, Devereux was back in England with his tail between his legs. He was further humiliated as he had been forced to leave behind his decimated army in tatters and was very lucky to escape with his own life. The queen was upset by this costly loss and the damage done both to her reputation and that of her country. And Robert Devereux's arrogant behaviour on his return did nothing to assuage her great disappointment in him. In fact it put him in a very dangerous position. In spite of their close friendship, she made her point by sending him to prison. Poor Devereux's situation did not improve two years later. The Earl, who had earlier enjoyed playing cards and even danced with the queen, was beheaded in the Tower of London. It is said to have taken three strokes of the executioner's axe to fully sever Devereux's head. It appears that, even in those days, a tough neck is not always a great gift.

In 1649, the Lord Lieutenant of Ireland, Oliver Cromwell, arrived in the bay during a violent storm. The purpose of this was to take vengeance against the Irish for their earlier attacks against Protestant settlers. On board his fleet he had with him 8,000 foot soldiers, 4,000 horses and a wide array of artillery. Dalkey Harbour would have been a very busy place. Violence was Cromwell's stock in trade as Ireland later learned at very great cost. A chilling example was when he and his forces massacred over 3,500 people in Drogheda, County Louth. His reputation in Scotland was no different, as the following year, in 1650, his troops slaughtered over 2,000 people in the coastal town of Dundee, and thousands of Scots were then shipped to the colonies as slaves.

In 1675 another Earl of Essex landed at Dalkey Harbour, this time as Lord Deputy. He was concerned at the sight of Spanish and French ships seen prowling along the coastline, posing a threat of attack and plunder. This gives us an appreciation of how coastal towns like Dalkey were so vulnerable to attack and needed to be wary at all times of passing ships and their intentions.

In 1726, the renowned poet, essayist and cleric Jonathan Swift returned home to Ireland from England and was met by a large flotilla of well-wishers in the bay. In 1751, it appeared that Dalkey might become the centre of a mining industry when lead and silver deposits were discovered. Small amounts of garnets were also found on nearby Killiney beach. Neither were viable for development and thankfully Dalkey was saved from the environmental destruction often caused by mining.

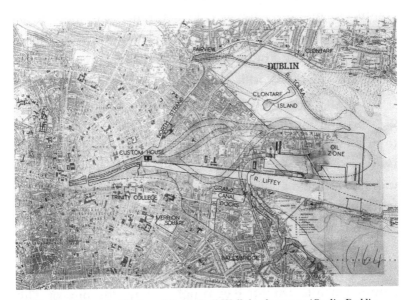

Dublin Port before the North and South Bull Wall developments (Credit: Dublin Port Archive)

Up to the year 1610, when the city of Dublin's Liffey quay embankment developments were commenced, visiting ships unloaded their cargoes along the rocky coast of Dalkey Harbour for later transport to the city of Dublin. Dalkey's seven castles in the meantime provided perfect storage and protection for them. In 1711, when the River Liffey's quayside construction was finally completed, all began to change. At that time there were three giant sand bars or large accumulations of sand in Dublin Bay, located close to the mouth of the River Liffey. All three posed a great hazard to heavier shipping attempting to enter. These giant sand banks were named the North Bull, South Bull and Kish Bank. In 1715, to help ships find their way through the sandbars and mud where the Liffey, Dodder and Tolka rivers entered Dublin Bay, large oak piles were driven into the riverbed and seabed to create a designated channel for shipping. This structure known as The Piles was completed in 1731. However, the entrance was still said to be far too dangerous for large ships carrying their valuable cargoes of wine, tea, brandy, salt, corn and other merchandise from around the world. Years of extensive dredging had failed to create a safe navigation channel. At low tide, depths of less than ten feet were not unusual. The oak piles, used to display the bodies of mutineers, Peter MacKinlie, George Gidley, Richard St Quinten and Andrew Zekerman in 1766, were the only aid available when trying to navigate all the way to the heart of the city, even if some ships could cope with the shallow depths.

In 1786 engineer William Chapman proposed the construction of a giant stone wall extending from the Liffey's mouth out into Dublin Bay, roughly along the line of The Piles. Such a wall would both protect the river mouth from

Kylemore Abbey in Connemara in County Galway - constructed in 1868 by Mitchell Henry with fine cut Dalkey granite

the south-east winds and help to prevent the build-up of sand across its mouth. Also, if successful, this South Bull Wall would mean goods would no longer have to be shipped to Dalkey, nine miles away by road.

Following the 1789 mutiny on his ship and having miraculously survived forty-eight days adrift in the South Pacific from Tahiti, Captain William Bligh of *Mutiny on the Bounty* fame and infamy was invited to Dublin by the director general of Inland Navigation. In September 1800, at the age of forty-six, Bligh arrived here. Reputed to have a very abusive and extravagant manner, he was to advise the authorities on resolving the debate that had festered for over thirty years on how to make Dublin Port safer for shipping once and for all. His brilliant navigation and surveying skills were well known, but this was to be a different challenge for the man who had served time under the famous Captain James Cook in the Pacific.

Bligh's assignment was to carry out what turned out to be a year-long detailed scientific survey of the bay, thought to be the first of its kind. He also surveyed Dalkey Sound, including the area around the Muglins.

Bligh eventually put forward proposals on how Dublin could at last be transformed into a safe asylum port. Applying his navigational, cartography and marine surveying skills, what finally resulted was the construction of the South Bull Wall and the North Bull Wall. The challenge was to narrow the opening where the Liffey, Dodder and Tolka rivers entered the bay, harnessing their combined power to funnel their enormous energy and to burst straight through the mud and giant sandbar that extended across its entire mouth. Huge amounts of granite to be quarried from Dalkey would also be required to construct these two protective walls that would create this powerful funnel effect.

The proposal was quickly approved by the director general of Inland Navigation in August 1801. Thankfully Bligh's original drawings have been carefully preserved in the archives of Dublin Port Company. Today, they are working on scanning and cataloguing another 15,000 historical maps and drawings which will help historians to better understand the details of these significant port developments. When the South Bull Wall was finally completed in 1824, with its red-painted landmark Poolbeg Lighthouse at the entrance to the Port, it was the longest man-made sea wall in the world. The construction of the North Bull Wall was completed twenty-five years later, in 1820, opposite the existing great South Bull Wall.

This feat of engineering transformed Dublin from a shipping viewpoint. Ironically, while Dalkey had thrived as Dublin's port for centuries, Dalkey granite was used to construct that great South Bull Wall, which in turn allowed virtually all heavy sea traffic and trade to switch to the Liffey and the newly opened up and safer Dublin Port. This clear channel into the heart of the city was welcomed by all, except by the traders, tavern keepers and boat pilots of Dalkey.

A place of pilgrimage for centuries, the small islands along Dalkey's coastline and nearby granite outcrops, are clearly marked on Alexander Nimmo's map of 1823. The little islands of Maiden Rock, Clare Rock, Lamb Island, Dalkey Island and the Muglins, combine to form a natural and significant storm barrier along this coastline. The shelter which they provide, even today, is greatly valued by all who live near or visit this scenic area. The small jagged Muglins rocky outcrop is the most easterly and is clearly visible to both passing ships and Dalkey residents and visitors. The Muglins have been the scene of much calamity over the years. In 1873 a Captain Hutchinson was asked to provide a list of vessels lost on this rock and reported that a total of twelve ships had perished there. Two years later, in 1875, Vice Admiral Tarleton recommended that the Muglins be lighted to improve safety. The number of ships lost on this rock rose to thirteen by 1876. Today it is a very popular area for recreational divers.

Surprisingly, Dalkey Sound and the waters around that narrow channel between Coliemore Harbour and Dalkey Island have some of the deepest waters of Dublin Bay. In his paper *"A Historical Study of the Minor Harbours of the South-east of Ireland"*, William Spratt-Murphy includes a study of the waters in Dalkey Sound, which showed that in a location between Sorrento Point and the island, a depth of almost 50 ft is available for anchorage. Considering that the entrance to Dublin port through the challenging sand bars was less than 10 ft before the construction of the North and South Bull Walls, the sheltered Dalkey Sound location was a priceless asset for the town. This confirms a vital reason for its significance over the centuries. Bligh was not the only one to consider Dalkey Sound as a possible site for a safe harbour. The Committee of Inland Navigation closely examined this possibility before Dún Laoghaire Harbour's construction began on 31 May 1817 at a time when a sheltered landing place was desperately needed. With the southern entrance of Dalkey Sound over 1,000 ft wide and the northern entrance 700 ft broad, plans were drawn up by Sir Thomas Page and the committee to:

> [...] run out a rampart at the south of the island about 100 yards long to break off the heavy sea coming from the south-east and building a good pier from the centre of the island into the Sound, about 100 yards on each side of which vessels may lie according to the winds.

The proposed pier would divide the length of the sound into two parts, with a passage of 700 ft wide at its end. However, after serious debate and much consideration, the project was abandoned in favour of the construction of nearby Dún Laoghaire Harbour. Again, quarried Dalkey granite and over 1,000 labourers were essential for this enormous project. The construction of Dún Laoghaire Harbour, which commenced in 1817, was completed in 1842, exactly twenty-five years after the foundation stone was laid.

At that time, many felt that this was a major mistake and that Dalkey Sound would have been the better alternative for a harbour as it was protected by the natural offshore rock formations of Dalkey Island, Maiden Rock, Lamb Island, Clare Rock and the Muglins, referred to by some at that time as the Strait of Saint Benedict. The issue raised its head again following the ferocious storms of 1861, when, on 9 February Captain John Boyd of the Royal Naval guard-ship HMS *Ajax* and five members of his crew drowned while trying to save those onboard the brig *Neptune* as it was being blown on to the back of Dún Laoghaire's new East Pier. Ten on the Neptune also lost their lives. This tragedy was all the more appalling as the drownings were witnessed by members of the public

The Muglins rock today with the small lighthouse constructed in 1879 – the site of thirteen shipwrecks off Dalkey Island   Credit: John Fahy Photographer

who were standing along the new pier wall. They could hear the screams of the unfortunate victims as they lost their lives. At that same time, conditions in Dalkey Sound were relatively calm and safe, confirming for some that it may have been a wiser and far less costly choice.

With even a little knowledge of the history of the Dalkey area and the large fleets that moored here over the centuries, you could be forgiven for letting your imagination run wild while enjoying the views of Dalkey Island and the Muglins rocks beyond. Seeing a small island just a stone's throw away, where the Vikings once ran a slave-trading post, where the granite walls of the old church of Saint Begnet, dating from the eleventh century, still stand and where the canon tracks on the roof of the 1804 Martello tower are still awaiting the arrival of Napoleon's forces – it would make anybody feel an observer of living history.

The three small rocky outcrops within easy reach of Dalkey Island are today nesting places for rare Arctic terns, cormorants and gulls, and are even home to very large harbour seals. Birdwatchers spend endless hours monitoring the nesting and migration patterns. Feral goats, first introduced by soldiers based on Dalkey Island during the 1803–15 Napoleonic wars, still thrive there today.

In 1849, historic experiments were carried out both on Killiney beach and Dalkey Island by Irishman and geophysicist Robert Mallet, a graduate of Trinity College Dublin. Using explosives and measuring instruments as his tools, he is credited with coining the words "seismology" and "epicentre" in his paper "On the Dynamics of Earthquakes". He is now regarded as the founder of the science of seismology and is widely regarded as its father. Mallet was also involved in the construction of the spectacular Fastnet Rock Lighthouse off Ireland's south coast.

While geophysicist Robert Mallet was creating tremors on Killiney beach in 1849, Queen Victoria arrived in Dublin Bay on 5 August of that same year. Her royal squadron comprised ten war steamers at a time when sail power was then diminishing. Each vessel in her fleet was illuminated at night, a sight not seen in Ireland before.

So the town of Dalkey, Dalkey Harbour, Dalkey Island and its surrounding areas, all played a pivotal role in Ireland's long maritime history, witnessed some extraordinary naval sights and in many ways, were Ireland's gateway to the world even before the Liffey was made safe for ships to enter Dublin Port and the heart of the city – all using Dalkey granite.

REFERENCES

A Biographical Dictionary of Eminent Scotsmen – Robert Chambers

Berrow's Worcester Journal – 26 December 1765

Blackrock, Dún Laoghaire and Dalkey – Tom Roche and Ken Finlay

Bulloch Harbour, Dalkey, County Dublin – Donal Smyth

Commissioners of Irish Lights – Muglins Lighthouse

Dalkey, a Guide to Its History – Michael Simmonds

Dalkey, County Dublin – Conan Kennedy

Dublin Port Company – Bullock 200 Lecture Series 2019

Enemy of all Mankind – Steven Johnson

Foxrock Local History Club, 1989

Historical Study of the Minor Harbours of the South-East of Ireland 2015 – William Spratt-Murphy, 2015

Historyireland.com

HMS Unicorn Museum – Dundee, Scotland

Hollinshed's Chronicles of England, Scotland and Ireland

Irish Varieties – Gaskin's Irish Varieties of 1869

Journal of the Royal Historical and Archaeological Association of Ireland, Series 4, Vol. 8

Journals of the House of Commons – ref: papers / Port of Regeala of Gueder, P. 397

Lancelot's Island Journal – Isle of La Graciosa

Lloyd's Register – London

Lloyd's Register Foundation – Heritage & Education Centre

Maritime London – London

Memoria Digital de Canarias – Port Hillsborough location theories and debate

Murder Pamphlet – Richard St Quinten Confession of 1766

Old Dublin Society – Gerald J. Daly, November 1990

Old Dundee – Eric Eunson and Bill Early

Pirates of the Carraigín – David Kelly

Pirate Queen of Ireland – Anne Chambers

Royal College of Surgeons / London Metropolitan Archives – Victoria Rea

Royal Irish Academy - A *Short Account of the Barbarous Murder Committed on Board the Brig EARL OF SANDWICH* – Richard St Quinten

RRS Discovery – Dundee, Scotland

Speed under Sail During the Early Industrial Revolution – Morgan Kelly and Cormac Ó'Gráda, 2018

ScotlandsPeople - www.scotlandspeople.gov.uk

The 18th Century Pirates of the Muglins 1989 – Padraig Laffan

The Alliance of Pirates – Connie Kelleher

The Atlantic – Margot Livesy, November 1994

The Dundee Courier – 8 August 1911

The Gentleman's Magazine – April 1766

The History of the Discovery of the Canary Islands – George Glas

The Jute Industry – Verdant Works

The Little Book of Dalkey and Killiney – Hugh Oram

The Neighbourhood of Dublin 1912 – Weston St John Joyce

The Newgate Calendar – *Executed for Piracy and Murder*

The Republic of Pirates – Colin Woodard

tramoreshippwrecks.blogspot.com

University of Dundee, Scotland – Archive Services /
    Collections

University of St Andrews, Scotland – Julie Greenhill / Special
    Collections

Voyage of the Beagle – Charles Darwin

Where the Saints Trod in Great Britain – Paul E. Garrett

ACKNOWLEDGEMENTS

If there is an appropriate saying to support this book, it has to be the well-known African proverb, "If you want to go quickly, go alone, but if you want to go far, go together." The help and advice I have received from so many wise souls made this a very happy journey. Many of the wonderful details are theirs and all the errors are mine. I am especially grateful to historian David Kelly for generously sharing important references along the way and even spotting some historical errors before I updated the text. I also thank each and every one of the following:

Lar Joye – heritage director, Dublin Port Company

Eamon O'Reilly – chief executive, Dublin Port Company

Dr Elizabeth Shotton – assoc. professor, UCD School of
    Architecture

Dr Séamas Ó Maitiú – proofreader and historian

William Spratt-Murphy – architect and historian

Rob Goodbody – historian and historic building consultant

National Library of Ireland – particularly Nora Thornton of
    Map Resources

Royal Irish Academy

Dalkey Tidy Towns Group – all the volunteers unveiling
    Dalkey's history

John Fahy – Dalkey drone and landscape photographer

Robert Kelly – Dún Laoghaire photographer

David Kelly – early Irish history lecturer, writer and historian

Gareth Davies – Edinburgh research & guidance,
  edinburghexpert.com

University of Edinburgh, Scotland – Centre for Research
  Collections

University of Dundee – Archive Services

Iain Milne – Heritage Department, Royal College of
  Physicians of Edinburgh

The Club Gastro Pub Dalkey (est. 1840) / community
  morgue – local history

Steven O'Reilly – Institute of Art, Design and Technology,
  Dún Laoghaire

St Andrews Parish Church – Dundee, Scotland

The Howff Cemetery & Parks Department – Dundee,
  Scotland

The McManus Art Gallery & Museum – The Howff, Dundee

Andrew Gritt - University of Central Lancashire /
  Representations of mariners and maritime communities,
  c.1750–1850

Valerie Kelly – IrelandXO Map

Joseph Hawkins – A History of a Voyage to the Coast of Africa
  1795

John Reid – Tenerife Private Tours, Canary Islands

Nick Ryan – Creative magic at Titan11Film.com

Ken Boyle – author and neighbour

Don Harper – designer, educator and steady hand, artwerkdh@gmail.com

Robert Doran – editor and patient advisor

Sam and Wendy Burke-Kennedy – for taking care of Covid-19 groceries

Mary Burke-Kennedy – text advice, typos and patience

ABOUT THE AUTHOR

Des Burke-Kennedy, BBS, MA, studied Business, Russian and Philosophy in Trinity College Dublin. With a strong interest in local history, he lives in Dalkey and his home overlooks the Muglin's Rock.

For more information, visit:

www.MurderMutinyandtheMuglins.com